HISTORY OF BEEKEEPING
IN BRITAIN

H. Malcolm Fraser.

THE BEEKEEPER'S CHARTER

This extract from the *Rectitudines Singularum Personarum*, written in A.D.1000, is reproduced by permission of the Master and Fellows of Corpus Christi College, Cambridge. The translation below has been made by F. S. Scott of the University of Sheffield.

Beo ceorle ʒe byreð ʒif he ʒafol heorde·
healt þ he fylle ðon lande ʒeræd beo·

mid us ıf ʒe ræd þ he fylle· v· fuſtraſ huniʒeſ to
ʒafole· Onſuman landū ʒebyreð mare ʒafol
ræden· Eac he fceal hpıltıdū ʒeara beon onma
neʒum peoрıcū to hlafordeſ pıllan· to eacan
benyрde ʒbedrıpe ʒmæd mæpecce· ʒ ʒyf he
pel ʒe lend bıð he fceal beon ʒe horſad þ he
maʒe to hlafordeſ feame þ fyllan· oððe fylf
lædan· ſрæðen hım man tœœ· ʒ fela ðınʒa
ſpaʒeрad man fceal don· eal ıcnu adellan
ne mæıʒ· ðonne hım ford fıð ʒebyrıʒe hede
fe hlaford ðæſ he lære bute hрœt frıʒeſ fy·

The beekeeper, if he has a taxable stock of bees, is to give (as rent) from it whatever is the custom of the area. With us it is the custom for him to pay 5 sesters of honey as rent. In some areas a greater rent is required. Moreover at certain times of the year he is to be employed on various duties at his lord's pleasure, particularly boon-ploughing, boon-reaping and mowing. And if he has good land he is to have a horse which he may provide for the lord's service or else lead himself, whichever is ordered. And (he is to do) various similar duties as is fitting. I am not able to enumerate them all. When he meets with death, his lord is to take charge of what he leaves, except for any freehold property that may be amongst it.

HISTORY OF BEEKEEPING
IN BRITAIN

BY

H. MALCOLM FRASER
B.A., Ph.D.

with eight illustrations and a bibliography

BEE RESEARCH ASSOCIATION LIMITED
678-680 Salisbury House, London Wall, London E.C.2
1958

by the same author

BEEKEEPING IN ANTIQUITY

University of London Press, 8/6d.

ANTON JANSCHA and THE 'ABHANDLUNGEN VON SCHWÄRMEN DER BIENEN'

Bee Research Association, 3/6d.

shortly to be published
by the Bee Research Association
as a companion volume to this book

BRITISH BEE BOOKS.   A BIBLIOGRAPHY
1500-1956

compiled by JOAN HARDING

Foreword to the 2002 Reprint.

IBRA is pleased that Malcolm Fraser's *History of Beekeeping in Britain*, which has long been out of print, is to be reprinted by Northern Bee Books. The book was in some sense a successor to his earlier work *Beekeeping in Antiquity*, first published in 1931. There was a second edition in 1951 which contained an appendix continuing the story from the classical period to the invention of printing. The preface to that edition stated that anyone who wished to pursue the subject further could obtain from the secretary of the Apis Club, for a shilling, a paper which carried the the history of beekeeping up to the year 1800.

It is interesting to note that in 1958 Bee Research Association was announcing that *British Bee Books. A Bibliography 1500-1956* was shortly to be published as a companion volume. In fact it was not until 1979 that IBRA was finally able to publish the *Bibliography*, with its date span extended to 1976. By that time much work had been done by others and Joan Harding its originator had been joined by three other contributors.

British Bee Books can still be obtained from I.B.R.A., so now at last the two companion volumes are available at the same time. They are an indispensable pair for anybody interested in British bee books and the history of beekeeping in Britain.

Dr Fraser in his preface mentions the records of the Manor Courts and asked readers who came across such entries to send him a copy of them. I.B.R.A. would be interested in receiving details of these and indeed any other records that are available.

David Smith, Secretary,
International Bee Research Association

This reprint of the 1958 edition was published in August 2010 by Northern Bee Books, Scout Bottom Farm, Mytholmroyd, Hebden Bridge, West Yorkshire HX7 5JS and printed by Lightning Source

ISBN 978-0-907908-76-0

CONTENTS

CONTENTS

LIST OF PLATES

FOREWORD

Beekeepers in many countries will welcome a new book from such a well known and distinguished authority as Dr. H. M. Fraser. The first major result of his researches into the history of beekeeping was the publication of his book *Beekeeping in Antiquity* in 1931, which established him as one of the foremost scholars in the field. His subsequent researches have been presented in numerous articles and lectures; Dr. Fraser has long been a familiar figure at International Congresses and at other gatherings of beekeepers, and many will recall with pleasure his lectures, in which learning and enthusiasm combined to charm his audiences.

It is curious that no previous book has been published on the history of beekeeping in Britain. Twenty years ago F. C. Pellett's *History of American Beekeeping* gave an account of the three centuries of beekeeping in the English-speaking part of America; but Dr. Fraser's book is the first to be devoted to the much longer history of beekeeping in Britain—which, until 1600, is part of the common heritage of this country and North America.

No one is better fitted to write this history than Dr. Fraser, and all those who have an interest in the subject will share my satisfaction that these results of his patient and discerning studies are now being published in book form.

EVA CRANE

PREFACE

For many years past articles have been published which deal with certain aspects of the beekeeping which has been carried on in these Islands from the earliest times. There has, however, been no attempt to produce a connected history of this beekeeping until the publication of a series of articles—on which this book is based—in *Bee World* during 1955, 1956 and 1957. Through the kindness of the Council of the Bee Research Association, and the untiring help of Dr. Crane, its Director, which the author most gratefully acknowledges, it is now possible to republish these articles in book form.

In this, as in all pioneer books, many shortcomings will be found. England is dealt with more fully than the other parts of the British Isles, about which less information is available. The subject is treated only from the literary side ; practical beekeeping is described from the books and documents which have come down to us from the various periods, and no attempt has been made to piece together the evidence from such ancient equipment and tools as still remain. Until recently there was in fact no representative collection of historical beekeeping material in the country, but the National Beekeeping Museum, founded by the Bee Research Association in 1953, has now collected together sufficient material to form the basis of a useful study. The practical historian of the future will, however, always be handicapped by the loss of the Royal Society's Museum, which was destroyed in the British Museum fire of 1731; amongst other treasures, this Museum contained Leeuwenhoek's original microscopes, with which his work on bees was done.

One additional source of information has recently become available, which has not so far been exploited — the records of the Manor Courts, which are now being collected together in authorized Depositories. It is likely that many of these records contain entries relating to bees, and the author would be most grateful if readers who come across such entries would send him a copy of them; they will be carefully preserved, and arrangements have been made whereby they, together with the rest of the author's beekeeping books and records, will be kept permanently in safe custody.

Suggestions for improvements in a second edition of this book will be welcomed, by both the author and the publishers.

H. M. FRASER

Cherry Trees
27 Elgood Avenue
Northwood, Middlesex

April 1958

CHAPTER I

BEEKEEPING BEFORE THE NORMAN CONQUEST: TO 1066

THE TIME BEFORE RECORDED HISTORY

Bees, if the truth be told, are secretive insects, not given to advertising themselves or their place of abode ; their habit of storing up honey and of stinging those who attempt to steal it must however have attracted to them the attention of mankind in very early times. Geologists have discovered remains of honeybees which they believe lived upon the earth some millions of years ago, and Indian beekeepers claim — with some reason — that the honeybee originated in their country, where three different species still exist.

There are legends which describe the introduction of bees into Ireland from Wales, and it is likely that some immigrants did take their bees with them, but there is no reason to believe that these were the first bees to enter Ireland, for the earliest record is of a land in which wild bees existed in numbers (Ransome, 1937).

Britain can therefore be imagined in the distant past as a land in which wild bees lived, were raided by their usual enemies—such as the bear and woodpecker—and if, as some tell us, the earliest Britons kept their cattle and other livestock in open country or in clearings in the woods, men would not systematically attack the bees, which were inhabitants of the forests.

How and when this halcyon state of affairs came to an end is not known; but at some period men started keeping bees in hives on their own land, and in the most primitive and out of the way parts of Europe, including places in the Alps, Southern Spain, the Pyrenees, the Biscay coast of France, Luxemburg, Denmark, Sweden and the British Isles, *small conical wicker* (or more rarely *bark*) *hives* still exist or died out quite recently. In eastern Europe, where forests of coniferous trees are common, *wooden hives* of various local patterns were used at an early date, but the area of their distribution was bounded on the west by that of *straw skeps* used by Germanic tribes west of the Elbe (and elsewhere), even before the

beginning of the Christian era (Armbruster, 1926 ; see also Fraser, 1950 ;
Berner, 1954).   The straw skep spread westward with the Germanic tribes
along the French Channel coast and north-west through Belgium, Holland
and Denmark to Sweden, and was brought to East Anglia by the Anglo-
Saxons.   On the French Channel coast the skeps were mounted on single
stools, but in Belgium they stood on benches under penthouse roofs ;
it is still possible to find these patterns in Normandy and on the Flanders
Coast respectively.

The foregoing tells us nothing about the earliest beekeeping in the
British Isles, but we know that until about 5000 B.C. France and England
were connected by land where the Straits of Dover now are, and that the
North Sea — which had earlier been dry land — was then shallower than
it is now, and it seems likely that the original wicker hives were at some
time brought over to these Islands from Europe.   Subsequent invaders
from the south or east would find the land becoming more hilly and
wooded as they advanced inland, and the people they met with would be
in an earlier state of civilization than those nearer the coast.   It now
remains to be seen what we can glean from the earliest British records of
beekeeping before these later invaders came.

THE ROMANS AND THEIR PREDECESSORS

Pytheas of Marseilles, who lived about 300 B.C., declared that the
inhabitants of Thule prepared a drink from grain and honey (see Strabo,
7 B.C.), and there are other early references to similar drinks in
northern Europe (Gayre, 1948), for instance to honey beer in Bavaria
about 1000 A.D.   Beer known as honey beer can even be bought in
Sheffield today.

Bees were found in Britain long before the Christian era, and therefore before the Romans occupied Britain, but no traces remain of bees and
beekeeping from pre-Roman times ; from the Roman occupation (43-410
A.D.) there is little enough — a small glass vessel containing honey which
was found in the Bartlow Hills (Ward, 1911, p.144), a few two-handled
honey jars (Duruz, 1953), and implements for writing on beeswax tablets.
Roman treatises on beekeeping (Fraser, 1951) give the impression that
the Romans were bee-owners rather than bee-keepers : the bees belonging
to a Roman's villa were kept in an enclosure and tended by a slave, the
mellarius.   This *mellarius* would assuredly, if he were brought to England
from Italy, find that the bees were different, that the season during which
honey could be obtained was much shorter and the winter much longer,
and that his hives and equipment were unsuited to the climate.   It therefore
seems quite possible that during the Roman occupation British slaves,
using their own methods, managed the bees of their Roman masters.

The question now arises : what methods were used in the British Isles before the Romans came ? A partial answer to this question can be given. Two collections of Laws have come down to us from ancient times and, as some deal with bees, they give us some inkling of the manner in which the bees were kept. The Ancient Laws of Ireland, which are the more important, consist of a collection of the judgments given by famous *brehons* (judges), which were regarded as having the force of law ; these Laws were codified in 438-441 A.D. by St. Patrick (who is said to have retained what was good and rejected what was bad), but they had accumulated over a long period and had not been subjected to Roman influence. The Ancient Laws of Wales represent another collection of laws unaffected by Roman influence.

THE ANCIENT LAWS OF IRELAND*

Hives

From these laws we learn that wild bees existed in the woods, but that there were also beekeepers who kept bees, often in their gardens which might contain a certain number of beehives. Hives are mentioned frequently, and in one place are referred to as ' baskets '; they were the ancient small, conical wicker hives which died out in Britain about 1885 (Watkins, 1920). These hives, though small (Plot, 1686), were very comfortable for the bees as the wicker work was ' cloomed ' with a mixture of lime and cowdung, which kept them warm and free from draughts, and the outside was covered with a hackle to keep off the rain.

Swarming

The colonies in these small hives seem to have swarmed three or four times a year. The queens cannot have been very prolific, however, since the dues payable on each hive were partly remitted during their first three years : ' the first year in which the bees generate, the second in which they are few in numbers, and the third in which they breed '.

There are mentions of dividing after-swarms amongst different people; this would seem to show a knowledge that casts often contain more than one queen, and an ability to divide such a swarm between the different queens. There is also a mention of the well-known ' white sheet ' used in hiving swarms.

Absconding swarms were frequent, and a reward was due to the man who followed and kept one in sight. Bees were frequently discovered in hollow trees, and many of these colonies were swarms which had

---

* These were published in six large volumes between 1865 and 1901. Volumes 1 and 2 contain a number of references to bees in connection with other animals or with people ; Volume 5 contains one reference only to bees, and Volume 4 includes a section entitled *Judgements concerning bees* ; Volume 6 is a glossary. In all volumes the Irish text is printed on the left-hand page and an English translation on the right.

absconded. The laws of property dealing with bees which had swarmed into hollow trees on land not belonging to their owner lead us to infer that the Ancient Irish found the difficulty of removing such bees almost insuperable.

Honey

Ireland at that time must have been good bee country, for it is only in productive regions that small hives can be kept in large numbers, and honey seems to have been plentiful. Amongst other penalties prescribed by the Laws for stinging by bees we find ' a man's full meal of honey ', which sounds a considerable amount.

The three types of vessel in which honey was stored were also of good size. A man could raise the smallest over his head when it was full of honey, the middle one up to his breast, and the largest to his waist only. There is one mention of a ship which was partly laden with honey.

Laws relating to bees and beekeeping

The legal position of the Irish beekeeper is difficult to assess ; the bees and their hive had a legal owner, but his rights were not those of the free and independent Saxon landowner. He was a member of a tribe, and his fellow tribesmen had rights over him and his property. A very severe fine (but not death as in some other laws) was inflicted on anyone who stole a hive of bees from an enclosed place ; it was a more serious matter to rob or steal a hive of bees kept in a garden than a hive standing unprotected on open ground.

The owner of the bees was held responsible for crimes committed by his bees, some being punished by fining him one or two hives stocked with bees. He was liable to pay compensation for any harm his bees did : in particular, as bees were in the habit of damaging fruit and flowers, he was compelled to pay a fixed share of his honey each year to the landowners whose farms surrounded his. This evil behaviour of the bees made it necessary to decide how far they travelled when engaged in these nefarious practices — it was decided that they travelled as far as the crowing of a cock or the sound of a church bell could be heard.

These old Irish bees must have been vicious at times, although it is noticeable that the Laws always appear to hold one bee accountable and to have no knowledge of mass attacks ; if a bee committed a crime such as killing or blinding a man or animal, it might be necessary to cast lots to determine from which hive the offender had come. The owner was required to pay a heavy fine for these or lesser injuries, but the penalty was considerably reduced if the injured person killed the offending bee. Apparently it was not known that bees normally die after stinging.

One difficult question has been left to the last. For certain offences committed by his bees a freeman (owner) was required to pay a penalty, but a slave paid nothing. This is understandable, but a stranger paid less than the freeman and a foreigner still less. Why were strangers and foreigners favoured ? It is hard to understand how strangers and foreigners came to be keeping bees in foreign territory, unless they were people who carried their bees from one crop to another, say to the heather. If this were so, they may have been given permission from the local tribe to bring their hives, and their bees thus given a qualified permission to sting. If this is correct, it is the earliest hint of migratory beekeeping in these Islands.

THE ANCIENT LAWS OF WALES

The Ancient Laws of Wales were codified by Howell the Good (918 A.D.), but are founded on much older material ; they are preserved in three editions, from North, South and South-East Wales. These Laws are neither a collection of precedents like those of Ireland, nor laws made by responsible authorities, such as the Saxon Kings. They record the customs regularly observed by the tribe, and as such customs grow very slowly, the Laws must have existed and been recognized for many years before they were committed to writing. Though they provide less information than the Irish Laws, they do to some extent confirm what we learn from them.

Mead and the Mead Brewer

Mead is dealt with at greater length than bees, beekeeping or honey. The King was to have a vat of mead from every free *maenol* [village] ; the vat must measure nine handbreadths ' in length diagonal '; if mead was not provided, there must be two vats of bragot or, failing that, four of ale. Some of the Welsh King's subjects were also required to hand their honey to the King or to the Mead Brewer on his behalf — the Mead Brewer being the eleventh man in the Kingdom. He was to have his land free, and his horse in attendance, his linen clothing from the Queen and his woollen clothing from the King, these being given to him at the three principal festivals. He had no appointed seat in the palace — his lodging was in the hall with the steward. He was ' protected ' from the time he began to make a vat of mead until he tied the cover over it. He was allowed a third of the wax left from his mead making, the remainder of the wax being divided into three parts, one going to the chamber and two to the hall.

It is specifically stated that ' the aillts [villeins] of the King are not to support the Mead Brewer, nor his household, and they are therefore not to retain their honey nor their fish but are to send them to the King's court ; and he may, if he will, make wears [weirs] upon their waters and take their hives.'

Swarms and swarming

These Welsh bees also swarmed a great deal, and the worth of the swarms was carefully documented :

B

An old stock 24d.
A first swarm 16d.
A bull swarm 12d.
A third swarm 8d.
A swarm from a first swarm 12d.
A swarm from a bull swarm 8d.

The passage continues ' If a hive swarm after August, it is 4d. in value ; and that is called a wing swarm. And so they continue [at the above values] until the calends of winter. From the calends [first day] of winter onwards each is an old stock ; and is 24d. in value, only a wing swarm does not become an old stock until the calends of May and then is 24d. in value'. The *alveary* [hive, presumably the small wicker hive] was worth 24d.

The mention of post-August swarms (and therefore the implication of swarms in August) supports the suggestion made when the Irish Laws were being discussed, that bees in Wales were then — as nowadays — taken to the heather : skep colonies at the heather still swarm frequently.

The only reference to property rights as they affect swarms is in a list of the ' three free hunts '. These were ' a swarm of bees on a bough, a fox, and an otter ; they are free because they are always on the move for they have no haunts '.

ANGLO-SAXON RECORDS

The Anglo-Saxon laws promulgated by their three Kings, Ina (*ca.* 700), Alfred (890) and Edward the Confessor (*ca.* 1050) dealt with the punishments which were to be inflicted on thieves who stole from bee-keepers, and had nothing to do with beekeeping except that they mentioned hives, and what must have been liquid honey, since it was measured in sextars and tubs.

In the *Rectitudines Singularum Personarum**, an Anglo-Saxon document dating from 1000 A.D. (Thorpe, 1840), the duties and privileges of the various grades of people who were bound to the land are defined ; the beekeeper and swineherd are grouped next to one another. The *beo-ceorl* and swineherd belong to the lowest rank of free men, and the *beo-ceorl* had to do all the work on his Lord's demesne land which other vassals had to do. He held his land by virtue of his office, and his bees reverted to his Lord at his death. If his land was good he was required to possess a horse ; this he took with him when he did his service on his Lord's demesne, to be used for haulage purposes. This information will be discussed when the Domesday evidence is considered (p. 20).

Anglo-Saxon literature contains many references to bees, but only a

---

* See Frontispiece

few tell us about beekeeping. A charm which was intended to prevent bees from swarming has been preserved (see Ransome, 1937) in which the bees are called *victor dames*. This, together with the use of the word *beo-mothor* which is also found in Old High German, shows that the Anglo-Saxons regarded the queen and workers as females. Drones do not seem to be mentioned. Honey and wax are referred to in wills, but wax is not mentioned in Anglo-Saxon documents until after the introduction of Christianity.

It is generally accepted as a fact that during the Anglo-Saxon period (410-1066) great quantities of honey were either collected from the woods or produced by domesticated bees, and that these ancestors of ours caroused nightly on draughts of mead brewed from this unfailing store. However when Wulfstan returned from his voyage to the Baltic he reported to King Alfred that : ' Estonia [Eastland] is very large — there is also very much honey and fishing. The King and the richest men drink mares' milk, but the poor and slaves drink mead. There is much strife among them. There is no ale brewed, but there is mead enough ' (Bosworth, 1859). Thus although there may have been a time during the Saxon period when England was ' a land of honey ', it seems reasonable to infer that wild honey, at all events, was in short supply in the more settled parts of England by the end of the ninth century (see also p. 21), since Estonian ' bee hunting ' was especially remarked upon by Wulfstan.

So far as the information available enables us to judge, the Anglo-Saxons had invaded a land in which beekeeping in wicker hives had been practised from time immemorial, having continued unchanged through the Roman occupation. Up to the present no evidence has been produced that the Anglo-Saxons themselves changed it in any way, except for the introduction of the straw skep in East Anglia (see Fraser, 1942).

CHAPTER II

BEEKEEPING IN THE MIDDLE AGES : 1066–1500

INTRODUCTION

During the four hundred years which this Section covers it may be said that beekeeping had no history — that is, if we regard history as being the record of the changes which men and their possessions undergo. At all events, it seems that bees were being kept in skeps in much the same way in 1500 as they had been in 1087. The descendant of the *beo-ceorl* was no longer a villein of low rank, but there is some reason to think he still looked after the bees in his district. England was short of wax (Rogers, 1866, p. 23) though there is some evidence to show that here, as in other countries, monasteries and nunneries kept bees to provide wax for lighting the houses and churches.

The Domesday Book provides a unique record of English life soon after 1066, and gives us some information about beekeeping at that time. Apart from this, the only way of obtaining a picture of beekeeping in the Middle Ages is first to collect the scanty evidence provided by books written during this period (discussed on pages 21–23), and then to gather together and arrange, as best one can, the scraps of information which have gradually been accumulated from very varied sources over the past thirty or forty years (pages 23–27).

THE DOMESDAY BOOK

Most people were taught in school that William the Conqueror ordered the Domesday book to be compiled in 1087, that this was done for taxation purposes, and that all possessions were so meticulously entered that no personal or landed possession escaped registration.

A closer acquaintance with Domesday shows that this was not altogether true. There was not one band of Commissioners but several, each with its scribe. Each of these bands toured the counties which were allotted to it, and collected evidence on oath from the inhabitants of each Hundred ; the scribe wrote this down on skins. These were transmitted to the King's scribes in London, who sorted, arranged and copied the information. The names of the landowners in each county were arranged in

PLATE 2. Wicker hive (see page 25), copied from the fourteenth-century Luttrell Psalter by Dorothy Hodges, and published with acknowledgement to the Trustees of the British Museum.

order, beginning with the King, and ending with such poor Saxons as the King in his mercy had allowed to retain some land. After the name of each tenant in chief is the list of his Manors, together with the account of what was taxable in each and its total value. If a man had several Manors in one Hundred they were grouped together. This information was supplied for three dates : ' T.R.E.', the day on which Edward the Confessor was alive and dead ; ' then ', when the Norman owner entered into possession ; and ' now ', the date of Domesday.

Domesday Book is in two volumes, not one : the Little Domesday, which was written first and contains the entries for Norfolk, Suffolk and Essex only, and the later Big Domesday which includes all the remaining counties of England over which William held sway at that time. The entries in the Little Domesday contain much more detail than do those in the other. Evidently the compilation of the Little Domesday took so long and entailed so much work, that less detailed entries were ordered to be made in the second volume. But when students speak of Domesday Book they refer to five volumes, not two ; the three additional volumes are known as The Exon Domesday, the *Inquisitio Eliensis* and the Bolden Book. The Exon Domesday is in the Chapter Library at Exeter, and experts believe that it consists of the very skins on which the scribe of the Commissioners for the south wrote down the information the Commissioners obtained. It is thought that after the completion of Domesday these skins were sent down to Exeter, where they have remained ever since. The *Inquisitio Eliensis* is a ' terrier ' — a list and particulars of an estate, in this case the estates which belonged to the Abbey of Ely ; Domesday scholars feel certain that the monk or monks who compiled it had been able to borrow the original Domesday skins of their district for the purpose. The Bolden Book is later ; it dates from 1181 and contains particulars of the lands of the Monastery of Durham, and is useful because at the time Domesday was compiled Durham was not included in the survey.

Beekeepers and their hives

Now that the meaning of the word ' Domesday Book ' is clear, it is possible to discuss such of its contents as relate to beekeeping. At Westbury in Wiltshire, nine *mellittarii* are mentioned, and five more were living at Lustleigh in Devonshire. Who these people were is not known. The name means ' honeyers ', and the scribe of the south-western Commissioners may have used it instead of *custos apium*, the usual word for the beekeeper (*beo-ceorl*) but, if so, one cannot understand why so many were collected at one spot. One suggestion is that they were people who collected wild honey in the woods : we cannot tell. A *custos apium* is mentioned in only two other places : Stocks in Shropshire, the entry merely stating that he was there, and Suckley in Herefordshire, where he is called the King's Beekeeper and had twelve *vascula* [small hives].

Ralph, the *custos apium* of Wolsingham in County Durham, is mentioned in the Bolden Book as holding six acres of land for his service in ' guarding ' the bees there.

In these entries the word used is *vascula*, a Latin diminutive meaning ' small hives '. In the eastern counties, where the number of hives is given for each Manor, the word used is *vasa apium* ; the difference seems to mean that in the western counties the small wicker hives were used (as they were until 1885), whilst in East Anglia and the counties covered by the *Inquisitio Eliensis* (Cambridge and Huntingdon) the straw skeps introduced by the Anglo-Saxons had superseded them ; these were of varying sizes, but larger than the wicker hives, a contemporary illustration of which is shown in Fig. 2.

In Suffolk *ruscae* are recorded, two at Winburgh and three at Campsey. These would seem to be wicker hives — perhaps the last remnants of those in use before the Saxon invasion. *Rusca* is the Latin word from which the French *ruche* is derived : it means literally a hive made of bark, and it is likely that before straw was available, bark was used for covering hives (see Armbruster, 1940, p. 38).*

In the Domesday records for East Anglia the number of hives recorded for each Manor is very small ; in many there are only two or three, and the greatest number appears to be 16 at Thaxted. Further, there seems to have been no difficulty in stating the number of hives on the three dates fixed by the Conqueror, and in some places the statement occurs that there were ' always ' so many hives. This seems to confirm the idea that — as until quite recently in East Anglia and as on the coast of Belgium even now — the hives stood on a bench under a penthouse roof.† This fixes an upper limit to the number of hives kept. Moreover the readiness with which the number of hives was given for the three dates suggests that they belonged to the Lord, whose bailiff kept accounts. There would be no registration of any hives belonging to the villeins, who did not pay taxes direct to the King — the Lord paid tax on all receipts to the Manor, including the rents and dues of the villeins. The numbers of hives registered in East Anglia were : Essex 615, Suffolk 359, Norfolk 467, total 1441 ; those in Essex have been listed in detail elsewhere (Fraser, 1953).

The beo-ceorl

The above may perhaps explain the position of the *beo-ceorl*. He came next to the swineherd, because as the swineherd looked after the pigs of the village, so the *beo-ceorl* cared for its bees. And if he looked after the hives owned by other villeins of the Manor, he might well need a horse to travel from one apiary to another. It is interesting to speculate whether

* The Agricultural Museum (*Landbrugsmuseet*) at Lyngby near Copenhagen has a *Kubehætte* (hive cover) of bark which came from Sweden.

† See Plate 3 (page 28)

the professional beekeepers of the nineteenth century were so to speak in direct descent from the Saxon *beo-ceorl* and the Norman *custos apium*. In the 1880s such an expert was hired by the Middlesex Beekeepers' Association each autumn ; he visited the members' apiaries and gave advice, and the members expected him to be prepared (on payment) to extract their honey and put their hives in order for the winter.

Dues of honey

The other entries in Domesday which relate to beekeeping are those which deal with customary dues paid by towns, and with wild honey collected from woods. There are not many references to wild honey, and they belong mainly to the west of the country. The dues seem to be pre-Christian, as they are always paid in honey, never in wax. Towns on the western side of England usually paid the sextars of honey for which they were liable, but the towns in the east commonly substituted a cash payment, suggesting that honey was scarce there (see p. 17).

BOOKS WHICH DEAL WITH BEES OR BEEKEEPING

Bestiaries

Englishmen have always delighted in the study of Natural History, and our Saxon forefathers translated into their own tongue some parts of a most uncritical Natural History, known as the Bestiary or *Physiologus*, which originated in Alexandria in the fifth century A.D. In the twelfth century bolder spirits, writing in Latin, ventured more widely and added further living creatures — amongst which was the bee. This does not mean that a scribe examined a bee or a hive of bees and wrote a description of what he saw — he had too much respect for learning to do that. He copied what was said about the bee in the *Origines* of St. Isidore of Seville (*ca.* 560-636), and added what he found in the *Hexameron* of St. Ambrose, Bishop of Milan (*c.* 340-397).

Books on husbandry

Paradoxically enough the following book is a fine example of the independence which characterizes the Briton. In the middle of the thirteenth century several books about husbandry, including Walter of Henley's *Husbandry*, were written (Lamond, 1890). Their authors showed their independence by writing in Norman French, and by describing husbandry as it was practised in England, not as the classical writers said it should be practised in Rome. Most of these writers say nothing about beekeeping, but the unknown author of *Ceo est hosebonderie* mentions it : ' Each hive of bees ought to give every year [swarms] for two hives on the average, for some give none, and others three or four a year. And in some places they are given nothing at all to eat in the winter, and in some they are fed ; and where they are fed it is possible to maintain eight hives right through the winter on a gallon of honey ; and if you collect the honey every other year, you would have two gallons of honey from each hive' (Lamond, 1890).

To the writer these words seem to have been written for the benefit of the housewife who kept an eye on the bees as she did on the fowls which lived close to her door. She was told how much honey to feed for winter (in the little hollow reeds which she pushed into the hive through the entrance), and how many swarms and how much honey should be obtained. from each. This is the sort of information she would need if she did not quite trust the professional beekeeper who attended to her bees, and suggests that the descendant of the Anglo-Saxon *beo-ceorl* may still have been carrying on this function.

Encyclopaedias

Two encyclopaedias of major importance were written by Englishmen in the Middle Ages. The first, *De Naturis Rerum*, was by Alexander Neckham (1157-1217), foster brother to Richard Coeur de Lion. This book was intended to be a compendium of the learning of the time, and so when discussing bees (Chapter 163) he turned for his information to Virgil's fourth Georgic and the *Origines* of St. Isidore. He must have read the latter in the original, not in the Bestiary, for his statement that bees sharpen their stings on their beaks does not occur in the Bestiary. Neckham mentions the generation of bees from oxen, and the bees supply him with many moral lessons : they begin life as legless grubs and finally rise to the possession of wings, they are chaste, obedient to their King, and have all things in common — they are in fact typical monks.

Bartholomaeus Anglicus, who wrote the other encyclopaedia about 1250, was an English friar who was summoned from his teaching in Paris to instruct the newly converted in the Province of Saxony ; for them he wrote his *De Proprietatibus Rerum*, which became so famous that it was one of the books lent out at a fixed price to students in the University in Paris. The English translation which went under the name of John of Trevisa was very popular in this country. Bartholomaeus' bee matter was much better than Neckham's, for he obtained his information from Aristotle whom he (like all the scholars of his time) read in a Latin translation of the Arabian edition produced by Avicenna the philosopher.

It is a pity from our point of view that these authors preferred to copy from ancient writers instead of using the material available in their own lands. It would have been much more useful to us if Neckham had given an account of skep beekeeping in England, and Bartholomaeus had described Saxon *Zeidlerei*.

Popular instruction

The Bestiary and the encyclopaedias were learned books ; the famous hermit, Richard Rolle of Hampole, near Doncaster, who lived in the first half of the fourteenth century, wrote for the ordinary man. He too used the bee as an example of virtue : ' The bee has three characteristics. One is that she is never idle, and she is against them that will not work, and casts them out and puts them away. Another is that when she flies she takes earth in her feet, that she be not lightly carried up in a puff of wind. The third is that she keeps her wings clean and bright.'

Very occasionally, learning unbent so far as to study the needs of those who knew no Latin, and about 1420 the agricultural works of Palladius were translated from Latin into English. One stanza runs :

> ' The Bee-yerd be not ferre, but faire asyde
> Gladsum, secrete, and hoote, alle from the wynde
> Square, and so bigge into hit that no thef stride.
> Thaire floures in coloures or her kynde
> In busshes, treen, and herbes thai may finde ;
> Herbe origane, and tyme, and violette,
> Eke affadille and savery therby sette.'

To sum up, it may be said that there is no literary evidence of any increase in the knowledge of bees and beekeeping between 1087 and 1500, but rather the reverse : the only way to obtain scientific knowledge of bees and beekeeping was to read a Latin translation of an Arabian version of Aristotle—from which a very small amount of new knowledge inserted by the Arabian philosopher might possibly be obtained.

CONTEMPORARY RECORDS

This Section will probably — and rightly — be dismissed as ' scrappy ', since the writer has been compelled to collect mere scraps of information from here, there and everywhere, and it has been impossible to weld them into a coherent whole.

On the whole the mediaeval beekeepers may be described as ' the world forgetting, by the world forgot '. Whereas today patents, grants, instruction and instructors, laws, and Orders in Council which have the force of laws, vex the anxious souls of beekeepers and those who manage their Associations, then, only one law affected the beekeepers—and that indirectly.   This was the famous Charter of the Forests of the ninth year of King Henry III (1225). By this law landowners were granted the ownership and the right of taking the wildstock in their own woods and forests.

As wild bees in a wood belonged to the owner of the wood, the taking of bees, wax or honey was as much an act of poaching as the killing or removing of deer, and it is to the credit both of landowners and tenants that cases arising from breaches of this law were usually settled amicably in the local Manor Court. The Court Rolls of the Manor of Patyngham in Staffordshire, for instance, contain frequent references to swarms *de extrahura* [stray swarms coming from outside the Manor], and also to swarms which had been taken by someone subject to the jurisdiction of the Court, and to the amounts paid in settlement of the Lord's claim to them.

Cases from legal records

However, even in those days, beekeepers did occasionally go to law. One interesting case was tried in 1457 (16 Ed IV), when William Mason sued Richard Ruddyng of Stonehale for damages for selling him a *cadum* of honey which was supposed to be pure, but was really impregnated with sulphur and other impurities. Ruddyng did not appear, and the Sheriff was ordered to arrest and produce him. As the damages claimed were 40 shillings, the cask was probably a full tun of 252 gallons.

In 1335 a case had been tried before the Justices in Eyre at Pickering (North Yorkshire), when Gilbert Ayton was charged with taking a gallon of honey and two pounds of wax out of an old tree trunk. Gilbert appeared by attorney, and claimed that, by the Great Charter of the Forest, every freeman might have the honey found in his own woods. The indictment itself stated that he had found the honey in his own woods of Bushell and Troutsdale, and he won his case. Those who took honey, especially from the Royal Forests, were not always so fortunate (Cox, 1905). In 1299 several men were presented at an Attachment Court of the Lancashire forests of Quernmore and Wyersdale, for taking a byke of wild bees and carrying the honey to the house of Ralph de Caton where it was found, and also for burning the oak tree which had contained the combs. The tree was valued at 4d. and the honey at 6d. Similarly in 1334, at an Eyre for Sherwood Forest held at Nottingham, two men who carried honey out of the forest were fined 12d., together with 6d., the value of the honey (Cox, 1905).

Other similar cases are on record, but it must not be thought that all mediaeval countrymen were poachers — most were good men who paid their dues. In the New Forest for instance, 6d. was obtained for honey found in the Battramsley Bailiwick in 1296. On the other hand the collectors themselves were not always law-abiding, for on 4th September 1490 the Verderers and Regarders of the Forest of Wilts. submitted that William Colwych, Forester, had embezzled two stalls of bees with their wax, value 5 shillings (Cox, 1905).

Other records

Besides the records of these cases, there are many other interesting documents. In some, wax was left by will, either as a yearly rent or as a specified amount to be used for candles for lighting a church — for instance in 1137 John, Archdeacon of Canterbury, bequeathed to Rochester Cathedral the rights and benefits of the Church of Finsbury and the Chapel of Strood, in order to provide wax tapers to burn continually on the altar.

Rents or portions of rents were often paid in wax, and agreements to that effect were solemnly made, often after years of argument. For example at the beginning of the reign of Edward I the nuns of Polesworth (Staffordshire) agreed to bring to the Church at Manceter 3 pounds of wax, and in 1254 Geoffrey de Bagshot held Chobham (Surrey) under the Abbot of Chertsey by payment (*inter alia*) of 12 gallons of honey valued at 6 shillings. At the same time the Vicar of Chobham paid 10 shillings and 6 pounds of wax. A plot of land 1¼ miles north-east of Chobham is still called the ' bee garden '.

One legal and one extra-legal record must end this list. On 25th August 1259 there was an Assize of Mead at Alrewas in Staffordshire. The extra-legal matter is William of Malmesbury's statement that, in the reign of Stephen, ' Robert Fitzhubert . . . used to expose his prisoners, naked and rubbed with honey, to the burning heat of the sun ; thereby exciting flies and other insects of that kind to sting them '.

Beekeeping practice

Little information is available about practical beekeeping during the Middle Ages. A number of illuminated manuscripts exist : some show wicker hives distinguished by their umbrella-like top stick, and others show straw skeps ; William Herrod-Hempsall has reproduced a number of these in his *Beekeeping New and Old*. Nowhere is there any mention of a log or wooden hive, but it is possible that hollow tree trunks containing bees were occasionally carried home. The instructions quoted on p. 21, and the mention that at Southampton (see Victoria County History, p. 455) half a gallon of honey already in store was kept for feeding in years when there was no new honey, make it certain that some colonies were fed for winter. Probably dilute honey in small quantities was put into the hollow stems of reeds, and these pushed into the hive at the flight hole. The case of Richard Ruddyng shows that sulphur was used for killing bees at least as early as 1457.

The statement ' Heath honey is the worst ' occurs a number of times (see, *e.g.*, Butler, 1634). Blends of heather and other honeys are usually considered pleasant to the taste, so these statements may refer to pure heather honey. If so, the honey must have been obtained either from bees in skeps which stood on a heather moor throughout the year (and which would be unlikely to survive there) or, what seems much more likely, from skeps taken to the heather. Of this practice no records before the time of Bonner (1795) are known to exist.

' Murrain ' recurring for a number of years and causing the loss of many skeps each year was recorded at Heacham in Norfolk (Harrod, 1867) and at Southampton (Victoria County History). It is impossible to write with certainty, but as European foul brood has existed in the New Forest for many years, there seems a distinct possibility that this was the disease at Southampton, and that both it and American foul brood already existed in this country in the Middle Ages.

A letter by Williams (1850) gives an account of the Officers of a Manor in Oxfordshire, dealing with the Manors of Aston and Cote in the Parish of Bampton ; after a reference to the *Rectitudines Singularum Personarum*, it is stated that a beekeeper was employed on one of the estates ; the Cote terrier mentions the ' bee furlong ' ; this sounds like a strip of ground where the hives were kept.

In the accounts of Oriel College, Oxford, and Sion College, Isleworth, there are a number of records of the purchase of hives at various dates at the end of the fifteenth and the beginning of the sixteenth centuries, at an average of about three pence each. Hive makers must therefore have been in existence then : it is possible that they were the successors of the Anglo-Saxon *beo-ceorls*.

Honey

The fact that sugar was not available in Britain during the Middle Ages is by no means conclusive proof that enormous quantities of honey were used and were therefore obtained by apiaries scattered everywhere over the face of the land. There is some evidence that more hives could be found in the villages in mediaeval than in Elizabethan times, but no numerical evidence for the whole country is available.

The dues of honey which are recorded in Domesday were payable in sextars ; the honey must therefore have been liquid. Armbruster (1926) believes this to be true all through the Middle Ages, as nearly all the records speak of barrels of honey, or other vessels suitable for holding liquids. Two reasons can be assigned for this : methods of storing, packing and conveying liquids had long been well understood, but the conveyance of comb honey in springless carts over rough roads must have been very difficult ; secondly, wax was more sought after than honey, and so the producers would find it paid them better to sell it separately.

This does not, however, mean that honey was never sold in the comb. Two instances are known (Rogers, 1866) of honey being sold by the *ruscha*. Although in Domesday *rusca* is undoubtedly used with the meaning of wicker hive, in one of these two instances the honey is stated to be ' wild ', which makes it fairly certain that these *ruschae* were baskets in which the honey was conveyed in the comb. There are also records of comb honey being sold at Oxford in 1473, 1479 and 1492, and at Selborne (Hants.) in 1451. It seems probable that this honey was produced locally.

Many sales of honey were reported ; usually it was sold by the tun of 252 gallons. The price varied a great deal at different times and in different places, but 3d. a gallon was a common price. The account books of the Monastery of Durham record the purchase and the purchase price of many barrels, and also payments to *portitores* who conveyed it from

Newcastle. In 1281 King Edward I and Queen Eleanor bought a quantity of honey at Conway Fair (Caernarvonshire) ; the cost was 1/4d., and the amount of honey was so large that a cart was hired to carry it to Rhuddlan Castle. Honey was sold at Conway Fair every year until 1954, when the harvest was so bad that there was none to sell.

Beeswax

The uses of wax and the records of its sale are also many. Edward I and Elizabeth, the second daughter of Henry VII, were buried in *cere* [waxed] cloths. Wax seals are well known, and so is the use of wax by the Church for making candles for burning in various ways. Church-wardens' accounts are known which tell of the purchase of wax for use at the great festivals of the Church. For some hundreds of years the price remained almost unaltered at about 6d. a pound, and 1d. a pound was usually charged for ' striking ' it, that is, making it into candles.

Agreements about rents payable partly in wax are common, and bequests of hives for the purpose of providing wax for churches have already been mentioned (p. 24). The writer would like to see a rule made to ensure that all future documents passing the Great Seal should be sealed with pure English wax. Owing to the present use of comb founda-tion, much less English wax is produced now than in the Middle Ages.

Wax was imported into England even during the Middle Ages. Rogers (1866) states that large quantities of wax from Livonia and other countries east of the Elbe were sold at English fairs during the Middle Ages, this being known as Boleyn or Poleyn wax.

Mead

About mead there is comparatively little to say ; as the honey required for its manufacture was easier to transport than the mead itself, and as every alehouse produced its own beer, it is most likely that what was produced was consumed on the spot. However the *Victoria County History of Hampshire* records that in 1296 there was excellent mead and metheglin at Southampton, and in 1291 30 gallons of methe are recorded in household accounts as having been received from Heckley.

Alexander Neckham (1157–1217) mentioned clare, which was a mixture of white wine with honey, sugar and certain spices, and also piment — a mixture of red wine, honey and spices, which was held in great esteem.

Looking back from 1500, at the end of the Middle Ages, we realize that beekeeping in the British Isles had remained virtually the same since the inhabitants had first learned to make hives, in spite of the radical changes which had taken place in the life of the country. It was not to remain static much longer.

CHAPTER III

BEEKEEPING IN TUDOR TIMES : 1500–1600

THE ADVENT OF PRINTING

At the beginning of the sixteenth century the art of printing was just passing out of the experimental stage ; by then it was possible to produce fairly large editions of books, and these could be sold at relatively cheap prices. Another important factor in the spread of knowledge at this time was the establishment of strong central governments in most of the countries of Europe, one result of which was an increase in the safety of travel. Authors could walk to neighbouring towns carrying their manuscripts to the printers ; horse-loads of books could be sent to distant parts of the country, and even beyond it, for customs duties were becoming less arbitrary than they had been.

Wherever books could be carried, men could journey, and the resultant exchange of information affected beekeepers as it did other people. This does not imply that a sudden crop of additional knowledge about bee-keeping sprang up, so to speak, overnight. However, comparison of a book written early in the century with one appearing just before its close will show that the manner of regarding our craft was changing, and this changed outlook was preparing men's minds for the great discoveries shortly to come.

LATIN BOOKS AND THEIR TRANSLATIONS

The first obvious duty of the printers was to help to spread the knowledge already recorded. Accordingly the works of Aristotle were amongst the first printed books, and to the early enquirers into the nature and life of the bee these works were more useful (being much more accurate) than the very early compilation *De re rustica* ; this was printed in 1470, and contained the agricultural works of Cato, Varro, Columella, Palladius and some minor authors. These authors were however read with great interest — indeed an English manuscript translation of Palladius had already been in circulation for nearly a century—for they dealt with practical beekeeping. Together with Virgil's *Georgic IV* and Pliny's *Natural history*, they provided some food for thought to many English farmers and beekeepers.

This the form ; a Frame standing on posts with one floor (if you would have it hold more Hives, two floores) boarded, laid on bearers and back posts covered over with boards, flat-wise.

Let the floors be without holes or clifts, lest in casting time

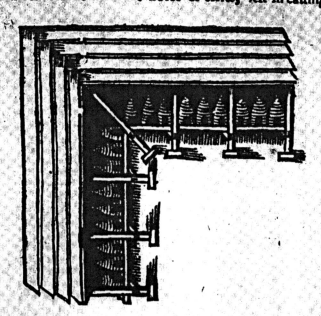

the Bees lye out and loyter.

And though your Hives stand within an handbredth the one of another, yet will Bees know their home.

In this frame may your Bees stand dry and warm, especially if you make doores like doores of windowes to shroud them in winter, as in an house: provided you leave the hives mouth open. I my self have devised such an house, and I find that it strength-ens my Bees much, and my hives will last six to one.

Hives.   Mr. *Markham* commends hives of wood ; I discommend them not : but straw hives are in use with us, and I think, with all the world, which I commend for nimblenesse, closenesse, warmenesse, and drynesse.   Bees love no externall motions or daubing, or such like. Sometimes occasion shall be offered to lift and turne hives, as shall appear hereafter.   One light entire hive

PLATE 3.   Straw hives under a penthouse roof, common in eastern England in Tudor times.   This illustration is taken from William Lawson's *Country housewifes garden* (1618); see page 33.

Three great encyclopaedias of agriculture appeared in Europe in the second half of the sixteenth century. These were the *Praedium rusticum* of Ch. Estienne (Paris, 1554) ; the *Pantopolion* of Georgius Pictorius (Basle, 1563) and the *Rei rusticae libri quattuor* of Conrad Heresbach (Cologne, 1570). The beekeeping sections aimed at adapting the Roman system to the needs of northern Europe. They were in wide use for a time, and all of them were translated into English. One other foreign book which had some influence on English beekeeping was the *Vinti giornate dell' agricoltura* [Twenty days of agriculture] by Agostino Gallo, which appeared in 1569. It dealt with the manner of keeping bees in Italy, and was in the form of a dialogue ; it seems probable that Levett (see page 31) copied his way of writing from this book.

It seems to the author that English beekeepers were determined to stick to their good old Saxon ways until something appeared which suited them better. In accordance with this we find that although the *Praedium rusticum* was translated into French in 1570 by Liebault, and successive French editions appeared until at least 1790, the English translation by Surflet in 1600 had no great success. Heresbach's book was translated into English by Barnaby Googe in 1577 ; another edition by Gervase Markham (1614) contained—as an inducement for people to purchase it — a statement that Markham had considerably improved the work.

Georgius Pictorius requires rather more discussion. In the first place Charles Butler (1634) stated that his book was the best of the three ; secondly it was the first of them to be translated into English ; thirdly it was the first book in English entirely devoted to bees. This came about in the following way. Thomas Hyll, Londoner — an author of astrological and other books — published in 1568 a translation of Georgius Pictorius under the title *The arte of gardening*, and in 1574 he republished the bee-keeping part, calling it *A profitable instruction of the perfite ordering of bees*. This book was successful (that is to say a number of copies are still in existence, so it must have sold fairly well), but it was not reprinted, and it had no direct effect on English beekeeping. Butler remarked very justly that Hyll had merely translated the best of the three foreign books, without making any acknowledgement.

THE FIRST BOOKS IN ENGLISH

In England Mayster Fitzherbarde published *The boke of hvsbandry* in 1523. It was the work of a learned man who wrote in English (although he inserted Latin tags), and dealt with husbandry as practised in England, beginning with ' Dyuers maners of plowes '. He wrote what an owner who employed a beekeeper to care for his bees [the descendant of the Anglo-Saxon *beo-ceorl?*] should and would know. He begins ' Of bees is lyttel charge but good attendaunce ', and goes on to talk of swarms, of hives, and of a bee called a drone which 'hath loste her stynge'. The whole article on beekeeping occupies 52 lines, over half of which are devoted to swarms.

The comparative neglect of bees by agricultural writers was continued by Thomas Tusser. In the 1571 edition of his *Fiue hundreth good points of husbandrie* he mentions bees only three times. In May, he warns the beekeeper to keep a good look out for swarms. In September, he says it is time for burning the bees and taking their produce, and he advises that driving, if done, should take place in June, and that the hives should be set on a plank, facing south, with boards to protect them from north and north-east. The final mention recommends feeding, where necessary, in December. Tusser, who farmed in East Anglia, seemed to expect the farmer to look after the bees himself.

In 1593 Edmund Southerne, Gent., published the first original English book on beekeeping : *A treatise concerning the right use and ordering of bees*. On the title page he declared war on the translations, and stated that his book was :

'Newlie made and set forth, according to the
Author's own experience : (which by any
heretofore hath not been done)'.

His advice *To the Reader* has been repeated by others. In June buy two hives and run two swarms into them ; at Bartholomew-tide you get your hives back, have some honey and also swarms. (Southerne was content to finish the sequence with eighty swarms.)

The book itself is not a systematic treatise on beekeeping. It contains simply what the author knew 'from experience', and he was wise enough not to talk about what he did not know. His knowledge was that of a person who owned bees but did not look after them. He explains where the hives should be placed and how they should stand, that hives must be small to ensure swarming, and that they must be dressed before use. The Ancients were demonstrably wrong in their account of the bees' method of breeding, but he cannot amend it ; he does however ridicule Hyll's instructions to kill the drones, and he rebukes English beekeepers for doing so.

Southerne has much to say about swarming, as might be expected ; he states that if two swarms unite they cannot be parted. The bees were not to be fed. Care had to be taken to close the entrances to one bee-way at Bartholomew-tide, and the hives were to be opened and spring-cleaned about the middle of April.

Those who read Southerne's book carefully will be able to form for themselves some idea of the method of beekeeping in England during the Middle Ages. The next Section shows that the book had considerable influence on the beekeepers who followed him.

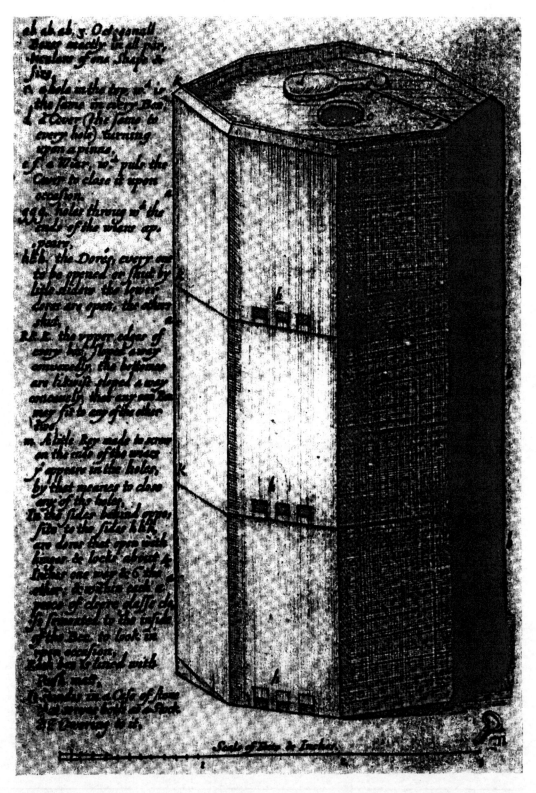

PLATE 4. Christopher Wren's drawing of Mew's hive, published in Hartlib's *Reformed commonwealth of bees* (1655) ; see page 35.

CHAPTER IV

BEEKEEPING UNDER THE STUARTS : 1600–1700

1600–1660 : THE FORMULATION OF BEEKEEPING PRACTICE

German books

The Latin books about beekeeping (page 28) had been superseded in at least one other country. In Germany, Nickel Jacob had written a book in 1568 which described the practices and knowledge of the *Zeidler*, who hollowed out cavities in the firs growing in their forests, and took honey from the bees which occupied them ; in some respects these *Zeidler* knew more than the Roman authors. Ten years later, in 1578, Eldingen published a book which dealt with skep beekeeping as practised on the Luneberg Heath, and which gives the impression that those beekeepers knew more about their art than their English contemporaries.

The first English book of the seventeenth century

John Levett published *The ordering of bees* in 1634. It was certainly written after 1600, because it refers to an event which occurred then, but it was probably written before 1609 because — according to Purchas (1657, p. 102) — Charles Butler had access to the manuscript before his own *Feminine monarchie* was published in that year. Purchas also states that it was written not by the John Levett who published it, but by his grandfather ; whoever wrote it evidently kept bees in East Anglia.

Levett was as independent as Southerne, but he knew much more about how bees were, and should be, kept. He had probably read *Vinti giornate dell' agricoltura* by Agostino Gallo (1569) and copied from it the dialogue method of writing. The book did not reach a second edition, although it promised to tell the reader much : ' The greatest use of this book will be for the unlearned and Country people, especially good women, who commonly in this Country take most care and regard of this kind of commodity (although much the worse for the poor bees) because sometimes they want help, sometimes diligence, but most times knowledge how to use them well '.

Levett adopted Southerne's attitude towards the Ancients, and he accepted some but not all of Southerne's teaching. He agrees that keeping

C   31

bees under a penthouse is not good practice, but he strongly supports spring feeding when necessary. It is impossible to read Southerne without coming to the conclusion that he had little or no knowledge of practical beekeeping ; on the other hand Levett knew what he was talking about — for example he points out that Southerne would never have rejected the existence of queens if he had ever seen a queen cell*, and that his idea of removing ekes at the end of the year was not practicable because the bees would have extended their combs to reach the floorboard. It can be said of Levett that he was the first English author who had a competent knowledge of bees, and his book provides important evidence in judging how far Butler's subsequent work was original, and how much was learnt from his predecessors.

Butler's ' Feminine Monarchie '

When one puts down Levett's book and reads Butler's *Feminine monarchie*, one seems to enter a new world. The cumbrous dialogue, with the wearisome exchanges of compliments between Petralba and Tortona, is replaced by straightforward narrative, which is much easier to read, although in the 1634 edition the orthography requires close attention. Further, the author is no amateur writer : he knows how to make a book and how to make it well. The conventions of the age demanded a *Dedication*, a *Letter to the reader*, and complimentary *Epistles* ; however when these have been read, what follows is a real book. It is divided into chapters, which are arranged in an orderly sequence and sub-divided into numbered paragraphs ; a short but adequate index refers to these and enables the reader to find the subject he requires. But this is not all : the writer was a learned man, who knew how a scholarly book should be arranged ; he used the margins of his pages for references which provide confirmation of his statements. Finally, the book is relieved by occasional lighter interludes such as the four pages of bee music — which were splendidly rendered by students from Worcester and Somerville Colleges, Oxford, when Butler's memorial window in his Church at Wootton St. Lawrence was unveiled on 14th November 1954.

The feminine monarchie contains much diverse material. New editions were published until late in the eighteenth century, and no English work on skep beekeeping has yet appeared which supersedes it. The material on skep beekeeping is found in Chapters 3, 5, 8 and 10 ; if we compare it with the works of Southerne and Levett, Butler's superiority is manifest — he has much more to say, and what he says is clear and correct.

The book does not deal with practical skep management only. It is a treatise on general beekeeping, and could even now be read with profit by a beginner. Butler, as his marginal references show, had read extensive-

*Crowninshield Smith (1831), from whom Langstroth learnt beekeeping, also denied the existence of queens.

ly, and the book contains some novel and original features, such as the description of the bee's external appearance and the detailed account of the preparation of honey, wax and mead ; there is also a great deal of ancient lore which appeared to Butler to be correct, together with modifications of some statements with which he could not agree.

Butler also published books on logic, music, English grammar, and the marriage of cousins. A biographical study of this versatile author is long overdue, probably because it would be difficult for one biographer to do justice to all his books.

Gervase Markham

So far this record of the seventeenth century has been one of progress in the management of bees ; they have become objects of interest to educated men, who were prepared to care for them as well as their knowledge allowed, and who were capable of studying them and of writing intelligently and carefully about them. Another kind of progress was by now inevitable—the emergence of the hack writer. Gervase Markham, who had failed as an original author, turned to the publication of books on horsemanship and agriculture (including beekeeping), which were of varying value. Markham's works made no attempt to reach the standard of Levett's or Butler's, but he published many books — which had a large circle of readers — and he adapted the contents of his books to their requirements. In his edition of Heresbach (1614) he gives directions for feeding bees, and recommends the use of new hives [skeps] ; he strongly disbelieves in driving. It is noteworthy that he devotes seven pages to bee plants. In his *Cheap and good husbandry* (which was his own work), the section on bees is entirely concerned with English beekeeping ; the hives are to be of straw or of wood (from the description these must be wicker hives), and the various forms of skeps known to him are described.

William Lawson

From Markham, the first hack writer about bees, we turn to William Lawson, the first of a long line of gardeners who wrote books about bees as well as about gardening. In 1618 he published *A new orchard and garden* and *The country housewife's garden*. Lawson lived in Yorkshire, on the East Coast. He used high conical hives, which an illustration (reproduced in Plate 3, page 28) shows standing on benches under a penthouse, against a warm dry wall in the orchard. He describes a tool he had invented to use when driving bees ; he gives directions for taking the honey and straining it, and remarks that if clean water is used for drowning the bees, it will make excellent botchet [mead]. Lawson's second book opens with the remark : ' I will not account her any of my good House-wives, that wanteth either bees, or skilfulness about them '; this makes it clear that small farmers and cottagers were now keeping bees, and wanted books written from their point of view. It was altogether a period when practical bee-keeping, not science, was the chief interest.

Moufet's ' The theater of insects '

Konrad von Gesner, the famous Swiss zoologist, died in 1565, leaving behind him an unfinished book on the natural history of insects. This passed through the hands of Edward Wotton, Thomas Penny and Thomas Moufet [also Moffett, Muffet], all of whom made additions to it ; Moufet prepared it for publication but left it unpublished. It was finally published (in Latin) by Sir Theodore de Mayerne, a Swiss who was Court Physician to James I and Charles I. Levett's book was published in the same year (1634), and both books used the same frontispiece, a beautiful wicker skep standing on a single stool. In 1658 Topsel published a second edition of the *History of four-footed beasts and serpents* . . . translated from the works of Gesner, and included with it *The theater of insects* . . ., an English translation (the only one published) of the book prepared by Moufet. But the border of insects which had surrounded the skep on the frontispiece of the Latin edition had now disappeared, and was replaced by a new one. The description of the bee, which begins this book, was probably the work of Gesner, as it seems to be based on the information contained in classical works. The book is of great interest to students of entomology, but is of little value to beekeepers.

Richard Remnant

In 1637 Richard Remnant wrote a book of 39 pages entitled *A discourse or historie of bees* ; to this was attached another book which explained how to cure blasted wheat, hops, rye and fruit, and the causes of smutty wheat. Here was a man who put bees first and arable farming second ; he was an agricultural writer of a new kind — a trader — who said : 'But now how to make metheglin I purpose not to teach you, for it is part of my present trading, and, for my part I have a good store . . . I have both bought and sold bees to the value of a thousand pounds by the yeere, for divers yeeres together'. He was a Puritan who signed himself ' Thine in the Lord '. Remnant's book was far in advance of its time and, perhaps for that reason, was never reprinted. Remnant knew that the workers were females, for he had seen their genitals with a glass and remarked on their closeness to the sting ; this caused him to think that worker eggs were laid by workers. He said that drones were produced at the pleasure of the bees, and advocated the use of drone pots [traps] made of osier. He described how the queen of a swarm sometimes fell into the grass, and how honey thickened after being placed in the cells, the cells being not back to back but ' placed triangular '. Robbing was to be cured by flouring the robbers and then sticking a knife into their hive; the consequent outpouring of honey would occupy them at home. He knew American foul brood, which was to be dealt with by cutting out the diseased combs, and he recognized the difference between it and chilled brood, whose origin he understood.

The Civil War 1642–1649

During the Civil War the time passed peacefully enough in many parts of the country. When the Puritans finally triumphed, the local Parliamentary adherent did his best for his Royalist friends and neighbours, and they returned the kindness when the King came back in 1660. Improvements in farming and beekeeping could therefore continue, although no new beekeeping books appeared.

The farming and account books of Henry Best of Elmswell in Yorkshire (dated 1641) have been published, and they tell us a good deal about his beekeeping methods. Swarming is his first and most important subject, and it is noteworthy that he expects a swarm to appear within a fortnight of the coming abroad of the ' great bees '. Hives are normally to be of 17 or 18 wreathes [bands of straw], and an eke five wreathes. His directions for hiving a swarm include the white sheet and muggerwort, and he also gives very complete directions for driving, which he recommends more particularly ' when bees lie out and under their stool about midsummer time, and never offer to rise or swarm. . . .'.

When driving and when taking the honey, Best specifies the presence and the work of helpers. He explains how the maids are to dispose of the honey : into one tub the honey is wrung, and into the other (which should contain three gallons of pure water) goes all the dross of the hive and the spelks — this is the first stage in making the three gallons of good mead which should be obtained from each hive.

The Commonwealth and Protectorate 1649–1660

Readers might expect that, after the absence of new books about bees during the Civil War, a spate of new books and new ideas would mark the restoration of peace. In point of fact, this was not so, but one great and far-reaching idea, which seems to have been purely English, did mark the beginning of the Puritan regime ; it was one result of the interest which the Puritan government showed in agriculture. This innovation was the honey chamber or super, which suffered a temporary eclipse in the middle of the eighteenth century, but reappeared later and made possible the full utilization of Langstroth's movable-frame hive, with all its advantages.

When the Reverend William Mew, of Eastlington in Gloucestershire, went to London in 1649 to take part in the meetings of the Westminster Assembly of Divines, he left behind him the design of an octagonal hive with supers.* On his return in 1652, he found that his wife had caused a hive of this design to be made and erected in the rectory garden. This information is to be found in Hartlib's *Reformed commonwealth of bees*

* See Plate 4 (page 31)

(1655). It is possible to infer that William Mew's son, Samuel, took the secret to Oxford with him, for it is known that the Master of Wadham, Dr. Wilkins, had such a hive in his garden. Moreover Christopher Wren, then at All Souls, sent Hartlib a sketch of the hive ; this was printed in the *Reformed commonwealth* together with the flowery and complimentary letter in which William Mew had given Hartlib all possible information about the hive — except its design, which of course was what Hartlib wanted. This design of hive attained a certain amount of popularity, for Pepys, Evelyn and Hooke all knew about it, and possessed hives of the same pattern. Hartlib's book also contains pictures of a long recumbent hive, which could be extended lengthwise when required, and of an upright hive shaped rather like a barrel ; this could also be supered.

The reformed common-wealth of bees may be fairly regarded as the first Government publication on beekeeping. Hartlib's work was subsidized by the Government ; he does not seem to have had any special knowledge of bees, but he collected from all available sources information which was not generally known. The book gives the information thus collected, but it has no discernable plan or order, and no recommendations are given to help the reader. The book begins by telling how a famous husbandman, old Mr. Carew of St. Anthony in Roseland, Cornwall, successfully produced bees from portions of oxen by Virgil's method. This is followed by the description of a hive made of a series of wooden hoops which fit one above another. After this, there is ' a translate of a letter written in High Dutch, communicating a Secret for the better ordering and preserving of Bees, practised beyond the Seas '—the planting of anise as forage for bees. The accounts of the recumbent hive and of Mew's hive are followed by philosophical letters, and recipes for making mead ; finally there is a list of bee books in English.

A comparison of this book with the same author's *Legacie* published in 1651 shows that the latter was a much more amateur production, in which he endeavoured to cover the whole field of husbandry without having made a real survey of it. With regard to bees, England is said to have a great deficiency as compared with cold countries, such as Muscovy, where much more honey was produced. Our beekeepers are also blamed for sulphuring their bees, for failing to keep them in hives made of boards, and for not making enough mead. Hartlib knew that bees were thriving very well in New England, and ascribed this to the presence of fir trees.

Commonwealth to Restoration, 1660

Hartlib's two books appear to have been part of an effort by the Commonwealth Government to restore, or perhaps to create, contacts between agriculturalists in this country and those on the Continent. This was an enlightened policy, but before it had time to take effect the monarchy was restored. This carried with it its own advantage, however —

the return to England of Royalists whose minds had been made more receptive of new ideas by a long sojourn abroad.

The Reverend Samuel Purchas provides us with a link between the Protectorate and the restored Monarchy. He was a duly ordained Church of England cleric, but during the Commonwealth he called himself the ' Pastor ' of his parish of Sutton in Essex, and shared the Puritan tendencies of most of the neighbouring incumbents. These two sides of Purchas appear in his book, *A theatre of politicall flying-insects*, published in 1657. At the end are three hundred short sermons which are very devout ; in the book itself we find a chapter which tells of the bees of America—perhaps a throw-back to Purchas's earlier days when he helped his father, also the Reverend Samuel Purchas, to compile *Purchas, his pilgrimes*.

The body of *A theatre of politicall flying-insects* contains the stock knowledge which might be expected, together with numerous references to the author's authorities after the manner of Butler. The most striking sections of the book are those which (although written in 1657) clearly foreshadow the days when bee science as well as practice would interest beekeepers. Purchas wrote about tree honey, and about insects related to the honeybees — wasps, hornets and bumble bees. He cut open the crops of sparrows which he saw eating his bees, and declared that he found therein nought but drones ; he discussed the breathing of bees, their blood and their hearts. Curiously enough, the scientists of the next period began with what seems to have been of little interest to Purchas — the bee's sting.

1660-1700 : THE FOUNDATION OF BEEKEEPING SCIENCE

Charles II, who became King at the Restoration in 1660, had spent a number of years in enforced travel abroad, and he was more aware than some of his predecessors of what was going on in the world around him. His Court included a number of intelligent men who were interested in natural phenomena, and a group of these men, headed by John Wilkins (later Bishop of Chester) who had kept one of Mew's hives in the garden of the Warden's Lodge at Wadham College, Oxford, founded the Royal Society in 1660. This group was responsible for a rapid extension of scientific knowledge, and beekeeping shared in this progress.

The coming of the microscope

By 1700 ten papers about bees, or containing important references to bees, had appeared in the *Philosophical Transactions of the Royal Society* ; there were six others of lesser importance. The first (dated 5th April 1665) was a review of the famous *Micrographia* by Robert Hooke, who subsequently became the Society's Secretary. This book contained a long description of the bee's sting and was accompanied by detailed drawings, which represented the first study of an internal organ of the bee made with a microscope. (In 1625, Prince Cesi in Rome had published a broadsheet containing three large-scale drawings of bees, and smaller illustrations of their tongues, legs, *etc.* — see Fraser, 1950).

These early papers also include a review of Swammerdam's *Historia insectorum generalis* (1669), two accounts of the work done by Leeuwenhoek (1673), and a review of the *Metamorphosis naturalis* of Goedartius. The third volume of this last book contains an account of bees, and has illustrations which are beautifully coloured by hand ; it is a real joy to possess a copy.

The invention of printing had enormously increased the dissemination of knowledge, and this had cleared up many misconceptions, and made way for new and more correct interpretations of facts already known, but the total stock of knowledge could only be added to by the aid of new tools. Two tools of fundamental importance — the telescope and the microscope — had been invented at the end of the sixteenth century. The telescope found its natural employment in the study of astronomy, and the microscope in the study of minute objects close at hand. Hence the possession of a microscope induced many scientists to study botany and entomology. Bees, which were more readily available than many other insects, and which were peculiarly interesting as the only insects used by man in Europe, were a favourite object of study, and the foundations of our present knowledge of their anatomy were thus laid. It is true that the first edition of Swammerdam's *Biblia naturae*, which was the only one published before 1700, contained no mention of bees. But the two papers by Leeuwenhoek (1673) dealt with bees, and it may fairly be said that when Swammerdam turned his attention to the study of bees, it gave a yield unequalled in any of his earlier work.

A further proof of the interest which scientific papers were arousing during this period was the publication of a compilation called a *Natural history*. This book, published in 1693, was compiled by Sir Thomas Pope Blount ; it was a collection of a large number of contemporary English scientific papers, a fair proportion of which were concerned with insects. Two of them were taken from Henry Power's *Experimental philosophy*, the first popular work about the microscope : ' The Bee ' and ' The mites or lice found on humble bees '. A comparison of Power's book with a mediaeval *Bestiary*, or with *The Green forest or naturall historie* which John Maplet published in 1567, shows how greatly science had advanced during the seventeenth century.

Science versus practice

Scientists and so-called practical men are apt to decry one another, although in point of fact they complement each other. The practical man, apt to denounce scientific studies — whose results he cannot foresee — is usually ready to make use of their results when available ; the chance, empirical discovery by the practical man, or the use to which he may put a scientific discovery, often opens the door to a new scientific investigation. We might therefore expect that the scientific progress of this period would be accompanied by a corresponding advance in practical beekeeping.

To a certain extent this was true, for great interest was being taken in practical beekeeping. Had there been an invention in practical beekeeping in any way comparable with that of the microscope, the advance there might have been equally rapid. But the new tools which had become available — the windows which allowed the interior of the hive to be seen, Mew's supered hives, the frames which Gedde inserted in them, and Wren's ' wier' (described by Hartlib) with which the supers were cut from the other parts of the hive like cheeses — made no difference to the fundamental principles of beekeeping.

The glass windows are unlikely to have revealed more than a close-packed mass of bees, and no discovery is recorded as having been made by their aid. Worlidge (1669) stated that the bees refused to make use of the frames which Gedde placed in his hives. Mew's supered hives brought three improvements : it was possible to remove upper supers and so obtain honey without killing the bees, the honey so removed was purer than that obtained from skeps, and it was unnecessary to kill the bees in well stored hives, since it was possible to remove some of the honey and yet leave enough to support the bees through the winter. Wren's wire, and the trap doors in the roofs of the supers, made these operations easier.

The foregoing paragraph does not take into account the following passage in Pepys' Diary (1665) : ' After dinner to Mr. Evelyn's ; he being abroad, we walked in his garden, and a lovely noble ground he hath indeed. And among other rarities, a hive of bees, so as being hived in glass, you may see the bees making their honey and combs mighty pleasantly.' This might mean that there was in existence a hive with walls of glass (not merely with windows in the walls). But even if such a hive did exist, it is unlikely that it would supply much information, as only the outer sides of the outermost combs would be visible. The interest of this arises from Réaumur's statement that Maraldi found single-comb observation hives in the garden of the French Royal Observatory when he moved to France in 1687.

Officially recognized beekeepers . . . .

The introduction to the first edition (1675) of John Gedde's *New discovery of an excellent method of bee-houses and colonies* contained the complaint that in No. 96 of the *Philosophical Transactions* (21st July 1673) the Royal Society had printed an account of the bee boxes for which the King had recently granted him a patent : this account the Society had obtained from Sir Robert Murray, who had received it from Sir William Thomson — to whom Gedde had communicated it for his private information. (Gedde had fought with Charles II in the Dunbar campaign, but had later fallen on evil times.)　The Royal Society acknowledged Gedde's claim, and he and his partners sold his pattern of hive for some years.　The hive resembled Mew's very closely, but a frame (to which the bees were supposed to attach their combs) was placed inside the boxes. Many manufacturing details — screws, pegs, glass windows, handles, *etc.*, were given in Gedde's book, of which three editions were published by 1677.　The boxes were to be enclosed in a special bee house.　This bee house was probably in the end their ruin : as a cupboard in which the boxes stood, it counteracted the thinness of the wood of which they were built, but it limited the number of hives, and was unhandy for manipulations.

To judge from the 1721 edition, Gedde's book was a considerable advance upon what had been previously published.　He borrowed from Purchas, Levett and Butler, but there was a good deal of new matter dealing with the internal anatomy of the bee.

In 1679 the sale of Gedde's hives was taken over by Moses Rusden, an apothecary who had been appointed King's Bee Master and who looked after the hives in St. James' Park.　His book, *A further discovery of bees* (1679), devotes about half its contents to the description of the hives and bee houses ; it is chiefly remembered because it stated boldly that the big bee in the hive was the King, and in the frontispiece depicted him adorned with a crown.

How Moses Rusden prospered we do not know, but in 1697 Gedde published the fourth (enlarged) edition of his book and revealed that the disturbances of the times had interfered with his business.　James II had renewed the patent, but William III did not do so.　No more is known of John Gedde, who was then approaching 70 years of age.

. . . . And their critics

After this account of what may be called the official beekeeping of the reign of Charles II, mention must be made of the ' opposition '.　J.W., Gent., (John Worlidge or Woolridge) earned recognition as a writer on agriculture and horticulture.　In his *Systema horticulturae* (1677), he attacked Gedde in these words : ' Many Attempts within these forty years have been made to keep Bees (those profitable Insects) in wooden Cases, and thereby annually to take their Honey, and yet preserve their Lives : Although the Invention, or rather Conceit, hath not yet succeeded yet hath the hopes of Gain prompted many to stock themselves with Bees, which design is now more likely than ever to be effected ; many ingenious men having undertaken at their own great cost and pains these last two years, are yet upon their Experiments to see the end of it : Very much to the Reputation and Advantage of him that gives them leave so to do.'　It seems, therefore, that there were influential persons interested in beekeeping and hive design, who felt that Gedde's patent checked their progress.

In his earlier *Systema agriculturae* (1669) Worlidge advocated separate stools, mentioned all the hives (including glass hives) which were known in England, and also the large hives, capable of containing 70 pounds of honey, which were taken to the buckwheat in Kempenland in Germany. In 1676 he published his *Vinetum Britannicum*, which deals with cider, and his *Apiarium* ; this reached a second edition in 1678. The *Apiarium* rather gives the impression that Worlidge did not know much about beekeeping, but he did invent and recommend an entirely new form of hive. This was to be a square box eight inches high and twelve inches wide and deep ; it had two doors, facing south-east and south-west, and two glass windows covered with shutters. When a hive was full, another with a small hole in the top was placed beneath it, and so on. The hives were to stand in a framework of wood to protect them from the rain ; the framework or bee house was to stand with one corner towards the south, and to have doors on all sides. These boxes do not appear to have been successful, for no more was heard of them.

Dr. Robert Plot, in his *Natural history of Oxfordshire* (1677), took a hand in the argument when he stated that one of the ' new sort of boxes ' had been set up in Wadham College Garden by Bishop Wilkins twenty years previously, and was still there ; he derided the pretensions of John Gedde and his seven years' experience. The same book contains an account of seven manipulations which two men claim to be able to carry out with skeps of bees. These manipulations could now be carried out only by well skilled beekeepers, and the first of them (the taking of swarms out of any stock that is able, and neglects to swarm) appears to show a working knowledge of Schirach's hypothesis that a colony with worker eggs can rear a new queen.

Plot also wrote a *Natural history of Staffordshire* (1686), in which he mentions basket hives as being found all over the county. He then calls attention to John Whitehall of Pipe Ridware, an ingenious man who had hives of many different patterns — more particularly square hives of brick with windows in the front and rear : ' within these squares of brick he sets his frames of wood, for the bees to work on, which he can take away as they work downward '.

A step toward the movable-frame hive

In 1682 Charles II knighted George Wheler, who had made a long journey into Greece and published an account of it in that year. To beekeepers the importance of this book depends upon Wheler's description of beekeeping in Greece, especially upon Mount Hymettus. He mentioned that the hives were usually kept at monasteries, and that as many as 5000 could be found in one apiary, the goodness of the honey, and the shape of the hives — these resembled wicker waste-paper baskets, with bars (to which the bees attached their combs) laid across the top, and with a conical roof and hackle. The most important statement was that, in the spring, the number of the hives was doubled by taking half the combs from each hive and placing them in an empty one. This statement attracted much attention at the time and was never forgotten; it may well have suggested to Wildman the cross-bars which he used in his skeps (1768), and so have paved the way for Langstroth's final solution of the problem of removing the bars and attached combs.

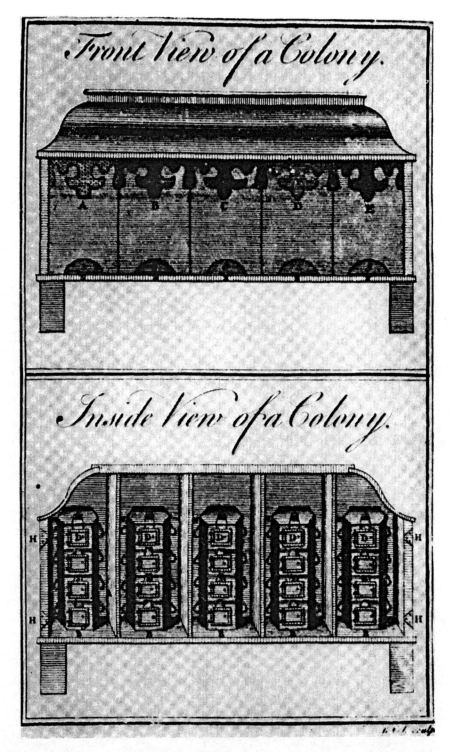

Front View of a Colony.

Inside View of a Colony.

PLATE 5. Drawings of octagonal wooden hives in a bee house, published in Thorley's *Melisselogia* (1744) ; see page 49.

CHAPTER V

BEEKEEPING FROM 1700 TO 1750

THE POSITION AT 1700

The commencement of the eighteenth century marked the beginning of a great change in the science of beekeeping, which slowly but steadily influenced practical beekeeping. In previous centuries books about beekeeping had been either founded upon tradition, or written by individuals out of their own experience and the knowledge embodied in the books of their own country ; these books were read by the author's fellow countrymen. As the eighteenth century advanced, communication between scientist beekeepers of different nationalities increased, and by the close of the century beekeeping science had become international. Had Swammerdam, who lived in the seventeenth century, read Remnant's book (published three years before the first edition of the *Biblia naturae*), he would in all probability have been led to discover the truth about the sex of the worker bee which actually eluded him. At the end of the eighteenth century, on the other hand, the alleged discovery of Schirach and the *Nouvelles observations sur les abeilles* of Huber were the subjects of sharp controversies in many lands. On the other hand the works of Anton Janscha, which were equally important, remained unknown outside his own country.

Towards the end of the seventeenth century England had for various reasons become the leading exponent of beekeeping science. Prince Cesi had done good work in Italy before his early death in 1625, but it was not appreciated until many years later. Swammerdam did no more work on insects after the autumn of 1670, and he died in 1680 ; if the second edition of his book (containing his studies of the bee) had been published soon after its preparation, instead of in 1737, the Dutch would have had at least a generation's lead in the study of bee anatomy. The Germans were long in following up the work of Nickel Jacob (1568) and Martin John (1684). However in England Butler's *Feminine monarchie* had been repeatedly reprinted, and had a number of successors ; the interest in beekeeping had been aided by Mew's invention of the octagonal hive and later by Worlidge's rival type, and also by the subsidy which the Commonwealth Government had granted to Hartlib, by Charles II's patronage of Gedde and Rusden, and by the foundation of the Royal Society—which not only included in its *Philosophical Transactions* beekeeping articles by English scientists, but also published in London the complete works of Malpighi and many of Leeuwenhoek's articles. (It is of interest that Leeuwenhoek left his microscopes and other material to the Royal Society, which kept them for many years in its Museum at Gresham College. The Museum was later transferred to the British Museum, and the collection was subsequently destroyed by fire.) By the end of the seventeenth century England was thus in a good position to take the lead in beekeeping science.

GENERAL TRENDS

In the eighteenth century the prominence of England in beekeeping science was paralleled by developments in practical beekeeping in Ireland and Scotland. In the second quarter of the century (1733) a book was published ' by Order of the Dublin Society ' which was definitely intended to help, and to be read by, the Irish. The Scots, who seem to have realized early the importance of beekeeping, produced a number of sound books at intervals during the century ; they dealt with practical beekeeping, and prepared the way for the outburst of scientific beekeeping literature early in the nineteenth century.

In England scientific papers on beekeeping were still published in the *Philosophical Transactions* of the Royal Society, but (with one or two notable exceptions) they do not appear to have been the work of experienced scientists, and they were not particularly important. The attempts to produce a type of hive which would supersede the straw skep were steadily continued. They were probably of more importance than appears at first sight, since the English books describing the new hives were translated into French and German, and thus influenced the work directed towards the same end which was being carried on in France and Germany.

At the very end of the century, the Western Apiarian Society was formed at Exeter ; it will be dealt with later. Meanwhile it must be remembered that — certainly in England, and to a less extent in the other countries which have been mentioned — the wicker hive was gradually disappearing, being worsted in a struggle for existence against better (but still not satisfactory) straw and wooden hives.

An anonymous translation of Columella, which was published in 1745, was a lone survivor from a past age ; it is worthy of note because it was the first and only translation of Columella into English until the recent volume in the Loeb Library. Columella was by far the most practical of the Roman authors on agriculture, but he seems to have had no influence on English agriculture or beekeeping. The translation is a fine quarto volume of about 600 pages, and makes it clear to the reader that Roman beekeeping was not based solely on the theory that bees could be raised from the carcase of an ox.

The history of agriculture in England between 1700 and 1750 shows that, on the whole, the period was an unfavourable one for beekeepers. The times were prosperous, and the population of the country was increasing ; new methods of farming — especially of arable farming — were being introduced, and country people were taking a keen interest in them and wanted to satisfy the increasing home demand for food. Bee-keeping, on the other hand, had not recovered economically from the drop in the demand for wax to make altar candles which followed the Reforma-tion, and increased foreign trade had led to the import of more foreign wine, which competed with the home-produced mead.

ENCYCLOPAEDIAS

The encyclopaedias of agriculture which made their appearance in England during this period confirm the above statements. *England's interest*, written by Sir Jonas Moore, a distinguished Civil Servant, was the first to be published. The earliest known copy is dated 1703 ; however, as the author died in 1679, it reflects the ideas of the days of Charles II, when beekeeping was more flourishing than agriculture in general. Accordingly a number of pages in this small book were allotted to beekeeping ; the author quoted Butler, and seems to have drawn partly on his own personal experience ; this was possibly gained in Hampshire, where he spent his later years, since he remarks that the Great Titmouse is called the bee biter in that county.

There are traces of a genuine interest in beekeeping in the first of the agricultural encyclopaedias which belong to the eighteenth century. This is the *Dictionarium rusticum*, first published in 1704 and ascribed to Nathaniel Bailey. Sixteen articles are devoted to bees, but none of them was specially written for the book ; those which dealt with practical beekeeping were carefully selected from sound, up-to-date writers, such as Worlidge and Hartlib. The lack of real interest in the bees themselves is shown by the account of *The generation of bees*, which explains how they can be raised from a carcase. Readers were told little about matters not likely to be economically profitable.

Three years later appeared *The whole art of husbandry* by John Mortimer, F.R.S.; he was a capable man, whose judgment was good, and the book was very successful : the sixth (and final) edition was published in 1761. It suited the outlook of its time, for like Bailey's book it specialized in practical matters. In fact the twenty pages which deal with bees (out of more than five hundred) are filled with material of the most hard-headed, practical nature. Worlidge is quoted twice, but most of the matter appears to be original. Mortimer was a confirmed skeppist ; like Gervase Markham he knew about driving bees, but he did not approve of it. He advises stuffing straw within the doors of a hive in cold weather. Of veils he says :

' The general practice now is to cover the face with black Italian crape, such as is used at funerals '. He makes two remarks about hives : ' Several sorts of hives are used in several countries ; but the general sort used in England are wicker hives made of privet, willow or harl daub'd with cow-dung tempered with dust, ashes or sand ' and, a little further on, ' The best hives and those that are most in use and warmest, are the straw hives '.

The clerical author, who is never long absent from bee literature, reappeared with the *New system of agriculture* by the Reverend John Laurence. This was a folio volume, published in 1726 and never reprinted. Seven of its pages are concerned with bees.

So far the encyclopaedias have shown clearly the tendency of the time. Agricultural improvements were being searched for eagerly, and there was a willingness to try practical suggestions for improving crops and animals, but chemistry was not sufficiently advanced to help arable farming. In beekeeping, science was more advanced ; however it had not yet reached the cottagers, and the octagonal hives were so expensive—and their advantages so problematical—that the only available means of improvement was the change from wicker to straw hives. Beekeeping therefore aroused little interest, and tended to be neglected by the authors of these books.

When a reader opens the *General treatise of agriculture* by Richard Bradley, and turns to the forty-one pages which are allotted to bees, he finds himself in a new, almost modern, atmosphere. Advice on beekeeping has almost entirely disappeared, and in its place is what might be described as a treatise on bee anatomy. The external and internal structure of queen, drone and worker are described from ' trunk ' to sting, and there follows an account of their lives from the time the egg is laid. Whence did Bradley, in 1726, obtain so much information which was entirely unknown to his countrymen ? The answer is simple. In 1712 the Italian astronomer Giacomo Maraldi had published his *Observations sur les abeilles*, and this contained nearly all the information given by Bradley. In 1742 an abridged English translation was published by John Martyn and Ephraim Chambers, but unfortunately no complete English translation of this valuable paper has ever appeared, although it contains the first accounts of many features of bee life which we now take for granted.

It might be thought that the encyclopaedias of the first half of the eighteenth century ended thus in a blaze of glory. However two very small undated books of this type were published about the year 1750. The first was an undated duodecimo of 165 pages by George Cooke : *The complete English farmer : or, Husbandry made perfectly easy in all its useful branches.* The author was a farmer at West End in Hertfordshire.

The second book (*Family pocket book* by Peregrine Montague) was also small, but it devoted four of its 162 pages to bees. On the whole these four pages contained sound advice—for instance pollen is needed for the young bees, and the best weather for beekeepers is that which is hot and calm with copious dews. However some of the statements sound strange to us : a distinction is made between white mead and strong mead ; wax scales are compared to a bird's feathers ; and—most startling of all—drones collect the honey from red trefoil.

GENERAL TREATISES ON BEEKEEPING

The encyclopaedias were in the main addressed to readers who regarded beekeeping, and agriculture in general, as a means of making money. We now turn to treatises on beekeeping, which were written for the benefit of the cultured middle-class reader who wanted to know not only what to do, but also why it should be done. The first was *The true Amazons* by Dr. Joseph Warder of Croydon. It was a famous and very successful book; the first edition was published in 1712, and the ninth and last in 1765. The seal of its success was the permission to dedicate the second edition to Queen Anne.

Warder's 'True Amazons'

This book was written before Maraldi's paper on the anatomy of bees was known in England, and a comparison between it and the preceding books helps us to understand how important this French paper was. Warder describes the worker bee in his first chapter, which gives a correct account so far as the external appearance can be observed without a microscope ; hairs are mentioned as visible only with a glass. In dealing with internal anatomy, he speaks of the sting and says it is hollow ; he says that a microscope will reveal the brain, and (in the breast) the heart and lungs ; that the flesh is reddish and fibrous and that the worker has a honey bag, and a gut with anus and sphincter. Moreover examination with the best glasses had convinced him that all the worker bees are females. He describes the drone, and gives the correct reasons for regarding it as a male. He says nothing about the queen until the middle of the book (where he describes at length an experiment he made to test the bees' loyalty to their queen). As he believed that all workers laid eggs, perhaps this omission seemed the wisest course to take. In the account of the life of the bee, Warder states correctly that three weeks elapsed between the laying of an egg and the emergence of the bee from her cell. The most notable observation is that which shows that he knew of the existence of malformed bees (1726 ed., p. 16); this is the first time such bees are mentioned and shows that Warder was a keen observer. Warder was a medical man, the first of many who have advanced the craft of beekeeping.

Warder recommended the use of wooden hives or boxes, which were to be kept in bee houses ; they were very like Gedde's. These hives were criticized by Thorley (who called to see Warder but failed to meet him); he said that Warder's colonies were weak, but he admitted that he saw

D

them after the honey had been taken ; he also objected to the painting of lions and tigers on the hives. This makes one wonder whether Warder had seen this done abroad. Warder's hives were also criticized in the book published in 1733 ' by order of the Dublin Society '.

Warder was a successful beekeeper, reputed to make £50 a year from his bees, and his book was well planned and readable.   Although small, it was well bound and attractive to people of the leisured classes.   Its success is significant, because it shows that the interest in beekeeping so apparent in the reign of Charles II still continued, although no general improvement in the art of beekeeping had yet been made.

The first Irish beekeeping book

The *Instructions for managing bees,* drawn up and published ' by Order of the Dublin Society ' in 1733 is frankly a compilation, intended to help farmers and others. It is an interesting book from several points of view. First, the Dublin Society was the leading Scientific Society in Ireland at the time, and the publication of the book shows that a number of important people there must have been interested in beekeeping and anxious to improve it ; these people had clearly studied the subject and were capable of forming their own conclusions on matters in dispute. They adopted Warder as their guide in describing the bees and, like him, they omitted any description of the queen. They were in general agreement with his methods, but they did not approve of his hives for three reasons : the expense, the liability to be severely stung when moving the boxes, and the bad colour of the wax, which was always two years old — ' Another inconvenience that attends Dr. Warder's Bee-Boxes, is, that by taking off only the upper-box yearly, The Wax in each Box will be two Years old, and consequently illcoloured, neither will the Honey be of that Year's gathering, by which means you never get the purest Honey or Wax.' So far as the writer's memory serves, this is the only book whose authors give a reason for preferring straw hives to wicker ones : the latter are said to be cold in winter and hot in summer. They were very firm advocates of the straw hive and the usual methods of managing it, including burning the bees, and they disregarded driving. They strongly recommend feeding, and a wooden hoop placed at the base of the hive made it possible to insert a plateful of honey below the combs ; Butler's idea of a gate for use in closing the hive when necessary was adopted, and this would prevent robbing after feeding. Finally the compilers designed a bee house which was cheap and likely to be serviceable in the damp Irish climate.

If this book is compared with the Ancient Laws of Ireland, it appears that bees were not kept quite so largely in 1733 as in the distant past, but the opinion was still held that Irish bees could collect large crops of honey, were rather quick tempered, and given to swarming. Unlike the Laws, the Dublin Society's book made no mention of wild bees.

Thorley's Melisselogia

Warder's book remained the standard English work on beekeeping until it was superseded in 1744 by *Melisselogia, or The female monarchy* by the Reverend John Thorley, a Presbyterian clergyman of Chipping Norton in Oxfordshire. The first impression the book gives is that one has returned to the Middle Ages : the author was a very pious man, and his book is full of moral lessons prompted by his thoughts about the bees. One is rather surprised to find remarks about our Good King (George II), but it must be borne in mind that the book was published in the year before the Young Pretender's invasion of England, and that the author of any book would be well advised to make his allegiance clear. Many copies of the first edition of the book are still in existence ; Thorley's son sold it at his shop opposite the Mansion House. Thorley himself had once been Chaplain to the Lord Mayor, and a long list of subscribers (many of them distinguished men) appears at the beginning of the book ; it appears to have been an immediate success. However the choice of illustrations seems to the writer regrettable. The frontispiece was a rough copy of Cesi's three bees — the first illustration (1625) of bees made with the aid of a microscope — used without acknowledgement. There is also an illustration of Thorley in his study ; the old man is seated at a table playing with his bees, and through the window a number of hives can be seen. These are straw skeps, standing on a bench — whereas Thorley recommends octagonal hives illustrated elsewhere in the book; one of these illustrations, reproduced in Plate 5 (page 43), is partly copied from Rusden's book.

Thorley knew the *Feminine monarchie* (he referred to the author as Dr. Butler), Rusden, Warder, the English translation of Pluche's *Spectacle de la nature*, Derham's *Physico-theology* and Baker's *Microscope made easy*, as well as the *Descrizzione dell'ape* in Stelluti's edition of Persius. His account of the anatomy of the bee was thus well up to date. He also settled the question of the sex of the queen bee by observing one which laid eggs as she ran across his hand. In addition he observed the wax ' plaits ' on the workers' abdomens, and gave their number correctly as eight. He considered that his great discovery was the use of fungus for stupefying the bees, and he made the first estimate of the weight of the bee by weighing and counting a swarm which he had stupefied in this way. His account of what happened when a swarm settled upon his serving maid shows that he was aware of the possibility of two queens being in one swarm, and that he was able to find the queen in a swarm — a feat beyond the power of most beekeepers of the present day.

A second edition was published by John Thorley's son in 1765. The frontispiece shows a new type of hive which the son had invented and was selling from an address in Lombard Street. The only other illustration in

this edition (and in the reprints of 1772 and 1774) shows a fanciful
' Chinese palace of bees '.

In 1745 an anonymous rascal went further than Thorley in using
previously published material, by printing a pirate edition of *Melisselogia*,
to which he added an Appendix containing matter from the English
translation of Bazin's *Histoire naturelle des abeilles*. This pirate edition,
in which Thorley's pious observations were omitted, was reprinted in
1760.

The beginning of Scottish beekeeping literature

Irish beekeeping literature began in 1733 with the book which had
been compiled by careful and capable members of the Dublin Society. In
the previous century two books had been produced by Scots, Gedde's
New discovery and John Reid's *Scots Gard'ner*, but neither can fairly be
described as a Scottish beekeeping book, and Robert Maxwell of Arkland
may rightly be called the progenitor of Scottish works on beekeeping.
Maxwell was the Secretary of the Highland Society, whose object was the
improvement of agriculture there. His book *The practical bee-master*, was
published in 1747, ' Wherein the management of Bees, both in Common
Hives, and in the Colony Way, without killing them for their Honey, is,
Step by Step, and on all probable Occurrences, better and more particularly
directed, than in any Book hitherto published.' A little further on he says
he wants to make understandable the discoveries of Réaumur and others.
In spite of this he thought the queen was a male, and that there were male
and female drones. He points out that Warder declared the workers to be
females, whereas Bazin (Réaumur) declared that they had no sex. He
adopted Pluche's statement that in Egypt bees were trained to obey a
whistle. A most important paragraph runs as follows : ' Now I proceed
to inform my Reader whereof the combs are made, which is out of a
substance they carry home in their bellies ; but whether this is a peculiar
juice they get in particular flowers, or if it is a composition of several
juices, so prepared in their bodies, as divests it of sweetness, and brings it to
a due Consistence, I shall not pretend to determine. Whatever it is, 'tis
plain they bring it out of their mouths, and apply it round the edge of the
cell, much in the same manner as the swallow puts the soft clay round the
brim of its nest when it builds it.' It would seem that Maxwell had observed, before Huber, that the bees lick the walls of the cells after they have
been completed.

SCIENTIFIC BOOKS AND TRANSLATIONS

Communication between the scientists of different nations had
recently increased, and the translations of foreign books on beekeeping
which were published between 1700 and 1750 dealt with the scientific
aspects of beekeeping. In order to obtain a clear idea of the advances in

this subject, the English books and the translations must be considered together. They will be dealt with in chronological order.

In 1713 the Reverend William Derham published his Boyle Lectures under the title *Physico-theology*, 'with . . . many curious observations,' including a detailed account of the stinging mechanism of the bee, with its 'two small, sharp, bearded spears'.

The *Philosophical Transactions* for 1721 contain a well known article by the Hon. Paul Dudley of Boston, U.S.A., in which he described and illustrated the method of discovering bee-trees and of dealing with them ; this type of bee hunting is still occasionally practised in New England. The article makes it clear that wild honeybees were plentiful in the forests near Boston in 1721 ; it is important in that it supplied most of the information which Smith Barton used in 1793 to show that the honeybee was not indigenous to North America.

Two translations of the *Spectacle de la nature* by N. A. de la Pluche were made between 1730 and 1740, the first by J. Humphreys and the second by Daniel Bellamy. This book was a popular treatise on science in the form of a dialogue ; on the whole the section on bees was not very remarkable, except for the statement that bees were trained to fly to pastures in which a whistle was blown, and to return to their hive when the whistle was blown there. This statement comes from the Commentary on Isaiah by Saint Cyril of Alexandria. De la Pluche writes as though Saint Cyril knew this to be true from his own experience, but the Commentary itself quotes the fact as well known, not as a personal observation. The anatomical descriptions were based on the discoveries of Maraldi, and so were up to date.

So far as the writer knows, no English translation has ever been published of Maraldi's paper *Observations sur les abeilles*, which he read to the *Academie royale des Sciences* in Paris in 1712. However, in 1742 John Martyn and Ephraim Chambers published an abridged translation, amongst summaries of other papers read to the *Academie* between 1699 and 1720.

In 1724 the Reverend Canon Derham described the mating of wasps in an article in the *Philosophical Transactions*, but he failed to draw the inference which would have solved the mystery of the mating of bees.

Mention has been made of the interest which English writers showed in the discoveries being made in France and Switzerland ; there has been little evidence so far that Englishmen were taking part in these observations. However a change began in 1742, when Henry Baker published his *Microscope made easy*. Baker was Daniel Defoe's son-in-law and collaborator, so a good sale for the book was assured. It was to be expected that, as a result of its publication, microscopes would become more popular and their owners would announce the results of their observations.

Then in 1744 an English translation of Bazin's *Histoire naturelle des abeilles* appeared ; in this book Bazin summarized in simple language the bee matter in Réaumur's *Mémoires pour servir à l'histoire des insectes*. Copies of the English translation are fairly easy to obtain, so its sale must have been good ; however no second edition is known.

One important result of this growing interest appeared in 1750 — the best piece of British work to be published in the *Philosophical Transactions* so far. Arthur Dobbs, the author of the paper, took as his main thesis the idea that wax consisted of the faeces of bees. In this he was hopelessly wrong, and disagreed with Réaumur ; however he rightly corrected Réaumur on another point, by insisting from his own observations that bees gathered pollen from one kind of flower only on each flight, and pointing out the disastrous cross-fertilization which would ensue if this were not so. He went on to state — this was the first discovery of the fact — that pollen is the ' male seed ' which fertilizes the ovum. As if this were not enough, Dobbs also gave the correct explanation of the function of the queen's spermatheca which, as he stated, Swammerdam had been unable to understand. We may fairly say that this paper is one of the most important, if not the most important, which appeared during the period 1700–1750.

POETRY

Purely didactic poetry rarely reaches a high level, and poetry which aims at describing bees and their management is no exception. Joshua Dinsdale, the author of *The modern art of breeding bees, a Poem* (1740) managed to write rather better poetry than his title leads us to expect. A few lines, taken at random, will give some idea of the whole :

> 'Twas thine [Virgil] to sing with next to Heavenly Art,
> 'Tis mine some new Discov'ries to impart.
> . . . .
> See how they light upon each Flow'r in view,
> And from the Calix suck the balmy Dew.
> . . . .
> And when no Nectar the scorch'd Flow'rs supply,
> Or waxen burthens for the gilded Thigh,
> They dawby Gums collect, and slimy Juice,
> Against the wintry cold of Sov'reign Use ;
> . . . .
> But if by Death to the Elysian Shade
> The much lamented Royal Ghost's conveyed ;
> In stately Pomp the honor'd body lies,
> And all the Hive is filled with mournful cries.

PROGRESS DURING THE HALF-CENTURY

The impressions which a study of this half-century have made upon us may be summed up as follows. Amongst practical writers the general assumption is that bees will be kept in straw hives and sulphured in the usual fashion ; wooden hives are for those who want fine honey and are prepared to pay for it. There was a notable improvement in the standard of knowledge found in the encyclopaedias and general bee books during the period, and a considerable body of middle-class people had arisen who were keenly interested in the science of beekeeping, and in the discoveries which were being made abroad. This interest had also spread to Scotland and Ireland.

CHAPTER VI

BEEKEEPING FROM 1750 TO 1800

GENERAL TRENDS

The second half of the eighteenth century was the period of the Grand Tour. Contact between individuals of different nations was becoming more frequent, and the Squire's son was likely to have seen something of the farm implements, cattle, crops and methods of agriculture used in various parts of Europe. This was not all ; it was the period which saw the digging of the great canals and the construction of the turnpike roads, manufacturers struggling to convey their finished goods to the nearest port where, in spite of constant wars, ships were ready to carry them anywhere — for improvements in ships and in navigation had opened all the oceans to their products.

Slowly, very slowly, this industrial revolution began to affect the countryside. The towns grew and absorbed more and more of the younger country folk, but the demand for English agricultural produce became ever larger, while the improvement of the roads made the carriage of food to the towns easier. So emigration to the towns did not prevent the growth of the rural population and, as always happens in an agricultural boom, improvements in cropping and breeding were pushed on by the insistent desire to produce more from each field.

How far did beekeeping share in this general desire for improvement ? At first sight one is tempted to say that little or nothing was being done. Beekeeping was still regarded as a side line from which the intelligent farm labourer who had a garden and an active wife might add a little to his income, especially if he followed the best advice and used straw hives. But this viewpoint does not give the whole picture. It pre-supposes that the scientific discoveries, and the improvements in the skill and methods of specialists, could never affect the ordinary practitioner, and this was certainly untrue. Encyclopaedias were still being published, and new ones replaced the old because they contained more and better information. The general treatises on beekeeping tended (though with some exceptions) to represent what was best in the thought of the time, rather than the interests and opinions of the

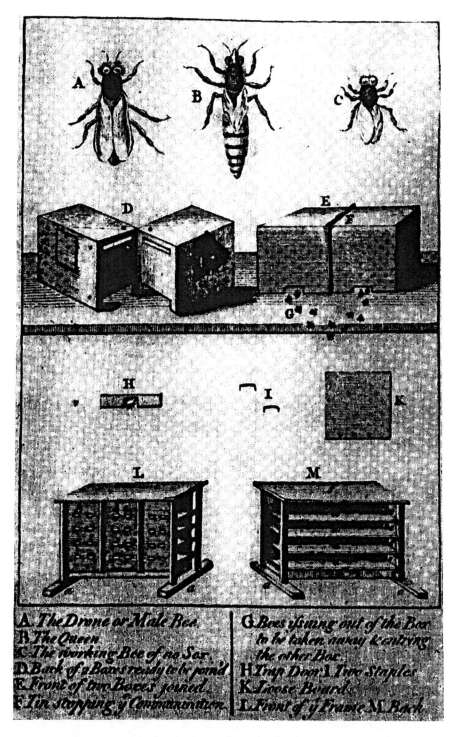

PLATE 6. Drawings of bees and of collateral bee boxes, from Thomas Wildman's *Treatise on the management of bees* (1768); see page 57.

author himself. The octagonal hive suffered a temporary eclipse, and left the way open for experiments along other lines. Scientific books and papers continued to appear, and — what was of more importance — all the writers showed some knowledge of the discoveries which the scientists had made. The most widely read magazines such as *The Scotsman* and *The Gentleman* opened their pages to discussions on bees and beekeeping. It seems justifiable to say — bearing in mind especially the denunciations of the sulphuring of bees — that there was a widespread desire for an improvement in the method of keeping bees, but no idea how it could be attained.

ENCYCLOPAEDIAS

The first encyclopaedia published after the middle of the century is a fine, large folio published in 1756, entitled *A compleat body of husbandry*. It was compiled from the papers left by a certain Thomas Hale, with additions by various other gentlemen. The title page declares that the book is founded on experience, and contains many valuable and useful discoveries never before published. Rather more than five of these folio pages are devoted to bees, which are treated in a sound, practical, and entirely English manner. The writer says that the drone and queen are male and female ; he cannot explain the existence of the workers ; he believes that wax is the faeces of the bees and that the dust on the lumps at the ends of the slender threads put forth by flowers impregnates the seeds — he probably knew of Arthur Dobbs' paper (1750).

The rest of the information is on severely practical skeppist lines. Feeding by means of small tubes is advised ; swarming, sulphuring and such matters are dealt with, and the writer notes that more colonies are lost during mild winters, when the bees fly frequently, than in winters when the cluster remains unbroken for long periods.

The encyclopaedias evidently filled a want, and two cheap ones — the anonymous *Farmer's wife*, and *The farmer* by Josiah Ringsted — were published about 1760 and in 1775 respectively. These small octavo volumes devoted about 12 pages to bee matters. The wording in each is identical ; it has not been copied from elsewhere wholesale, but it contains no original matter, and probably little importance was attached to beekeeping except in ensuring the completeness of the book. Although the text recommends that hives should be placed on separate stools, the frontispiece shows three skeps standing on a bench in an open-fronted shed.

BOOKS INTENDED TO ADVANCE PRACTICAL BEEKEEPING

Though one or two books on general beekeeping were published between 1750 and 1760, it seems right to deal with Mills' *Essay on the management of bees* (1766) at the beginning of this section. This may be described as an original book which contains nothing original : the book is a compilation, but no such compilation had been made for over a hundred years, and this *Essay* is really an encyclopaedia of beekeeping. In the 'Advertisement' at the beginning of the book, Mills states that it was originally intended to form part of his *System of practical husbandry* (of which five volumes had been published), but it was being published at once partly because of his ill-heath, and partly because the Society of Arts, Manufactures and Commerce desired to promote the 'Means of Saving the Lives of these useful Insects'.

Mills had read all the best English and foreign works about bees which were current at the time. His account of the formation of wax seems designedly ambiguous, but he summarized clearly the work of the Abbé Boissier de Sauvages on the nature and production of honeydew. The outline of anatomy with which he starts is correct as far as it goes ; it is interesting in that it is hard to trace the work of Maraldi elsewhere in the book. However, Mills kept in mind his object in writing the book, and therein lies its chief value. Amongst English hives the various forms of the octagonal hive, and White's collateral boxes (which had not long been invented), are mentioned — because from them honey could be obtained without killing the bees. After a short mention of M. Palteau's hive, he gives a full account of Madame Vicat and her work which, so far as the writer knows, can otherwise only be obtained by examining the original papers at Geneva. The importance of the work of de Gélieu and of Madame Vicat is well known ; de Gélieu's work was translated into English by Miss Stirling Graham, and some account of their lives will be found in Melchior Sooder's *Bienen und Bienenhalten in der Schweiz* (1952). In spite of the excellence of Mills' work, however, English writers continued to state firmly that 'straw hives are the best'.

A few years earlier (1756) the Reverend Stephen White had published a book which he called *Collateral bee-boxes*. These boxes were plain cubes of about 9 inches ; strips of wood were removed at the top and bottom of one side, to enable the bees to pass from one box to another placed beside it. When one box was used alone, this side (or sides, if both had strips cut out) was covered with a piece of board held in position by staples. The bees were supposed to use the central box as a brood chamber, and the side one or ones for storing honey. When the honey was to be removed, the board between the boxes was replaced ; those bees which were in the honey box then left it by its entrance and re-entered by the brood box, but were prevented by the board from reaching the honey box ; this could then be removed.

The hives were stacked in a covered frame in order to protect them from the weather.

White lived in a good district in Suffolk, and he probably collected sufficient honey to satisfy himself ; however his hives — though fashionable for a time — do not seem to have yielded big crops, and the system fell into disuse until Nutt revived it in the next century.

The ' bee masters '

Mention must now be made of a curious phenomenon which appeared about this time. In 1728 a certain Père Labat had published an account of a native he had met near the River Senegal, who was constantly accompanied by swarms of bees, and who claimed to be master of the bees ; the inference is that he carried the queen with him. Then in 1744 Thorley had described how he found and removed two queens from a swarm which had clustered on his maid's neck. In his own book Mills mentioned this, and stated that at Plymouth a man could do a similar thing. This man was Thomas Wildman, who lectured in London wearing a beard of bees, rode on horseback when covered with bees, and made bees run backward and forward from hive to hive. He was a charlatan, but he must have possessed great skill in finding the queen. In 1768 he published a book, *A treatise on the management of bees*, which he was allowed to dedicate to Queen Charlotte. Wildman was not a scientist, but his book shows a competent knowledge of beekeeping and is the work of an intelligent man who took an interest also in wasps and hornets ; he described the hives of previous English writers and of the Count de la Bourdonnaye and Madame Vicat. The hive which he recommended was very like that of the Count, but he says that he devised his own independently. Plate 6 (page 54) shows one of the plates from Wildman's book.

Wildman was interesting, especially as he was the first known bee expert to visit apiaries and look after his patrons' bees (he died when visiting a house where he attended to the bees) ; there must therefore have been gentry who were willing to pay for the services of a bee expert.

Daniel Wildman, Thomas' nephew, was also interested in bees and also wrote a book about them ; it was much smaller than his uncle's, and was published in 1773, only five years after the other ; it was entitled *A complete guide for the management of bees*. It went into many editions, for Daniel was a good business man. Like his uncle he gave performances with bees ; he seems to have travelled the Continent giving shows, and to have been roughly handled there by Johann Riem. However his main concern was his shop, No. 326 Holborn, near Gray's Inn, where he kept and sold bees and hives ; in accordance with his own idea, these mostly had flat tops with holes over which bottles and bell glasses could be placed, in which the bees placed pure, clean comb honey. Wildman is said to have desired to know how far his bees travelled in search of nectar, and to have floured some as they emerged from a hive in Holborn, subsequently finding them busy at Hampstead. To Thorley's son bees and hives were probably a side line ; Daniel Wildman may therefore be regarded as the first English professional beekeeping appliance maker.

ELEMENTARY BEEKEEPING BOOKS

In the last section we have considered books whose object was the improvement of practical beekeeping. There was however a continuous demand for simpler, if less up-to-date, text-books.

Samuel Cooke's ' Complete bee-master '

The man who first endeavoured to satisfy this demand was a certain Samuel Cooke, who included a *Complete bee-master* of 25 pages in his *Complete English gardener*. The book is undated, but each of the two copies I have seen contained the signature of the first owner and the date 1780. The only piece of original work in the bee matter appears to be the statement ' There are several sorts of hives used in several countries but those mostly used in England are wicker hives made of previt, willow or harl, daubed with cow dung, tempered with dust, ashes, or sand ; or hives made with straw bound with bramblets '. This was written from Overton in Wiltshire, and helps to explain the long continuance of wicker hives in England. Wiltshire was a grazing, not an arable county, and the beekeepers who made hives preferred wicker — which could be obtained locally — to straw, which came from a distance. Some idea of the hives of this time can be gathered from the statement : ' The warmest and best are made of straw between 5 and 7 gallons, of a round form, rather broad than high '.

William White

If the reader happens to be a collector of bee books, like the author, he may well succeed in obtaining a copy of William White's *Complete guide to the mystery and management of bees*. But it will probably be a copy, not of the original edition of 1771, but of a neat book printed in 1852 in the severely plain type which its printers had invented. However he may be comforted by discovering that *A practical monthly bee calendar* by a certain James Beesley of Banbury had been added.

White seems to have been a professional beekeeper ; he was given a premium by the Society of Arts and Sciences for his singular ability in beekeeping, and he seems to have known all the tricks of his trade. For example he was completely successful in removing a colony of bees from a hollow in a tree ; the process was simple — he put in his hand, took out the queen and placed her in a hive nearby.

Amongst other information a warning is found that if bees are kept in the hive all through the winter, they will be found dead and swollen in the spring. White kept young queens in boxes in his hives and fed them, and made artificial swarms in two ways : by driving, and removing the empty hive as soon as the queen went into it (leaving the remaining bees to raise a queen), and by securing the spare queens in casts ; each of them was used to start a new colony. He says that feeding should be done in April, and in May and June if larvae are being thrown out.

William White lived near Banbury in Oxfordshire, and a comparison of his exploits with those of the two beekeepers mentioned by Plot in his *Natural history of Oxfordshire* (referred to on page 41), makes it seem at least possible that professional descendents of the Saxon *beo-ceorls* still attended to their neighbours' bees, in that county at all events.

John Keys

A more important man, who may or may not have made his livelihood from his bees, was John Keys. He wrote his first book, *The practical bee-master*, when living in Cheshunt Street, Herts. He subsequently moved to Bee Hall near Pembroke ; this still exists, and the neighbours know that bees were once kept there. The move enabled him to compare the productivity of several different parts of the country. Rather strangely, Herefordshire is rated as a district yielding small honey crops, in spite of the large number of orchards there. In all probability the hives Keys saw wintered poorly and failed to take full advantage of the fruit blossom. He constrasts Herefordshire with the borders of Cambridgeshire and Hertfordshire, and that part of Hampshire which abounds in large heaths, commons and woods — this he regarded as much more productive than any other part of the kingdom. Again one suspects that Keys' colonies built up late ; it should be remembered too that Charles Butler, whose hives were in Hampshire, remarked that 'heath honey is the worst'; he may have harvested more of it than of any other.

A notable difference between the eastern and western sides of the country was in the size of swarms. In Pembrokeshire bees had been kept for hundreds of years in small wicker hives, and they produced swarms rarely exceeding a peck (6 lb. 5 oz., according to Keys) ; in Hertfordshire, where they were kept in large straw skeps, swarms were often twice this size — half a bushel or more. Twelve pounds seems a good size for a swarm, and one wonders if such swarms are common at the present time.

For the rest, Keys disliked Wildman and his advertising ways ; he disbelieved Schirach's theory that bees could raise queens from young worker larvae, because he had repeatedly tried to do this, but had always failed. James Bonner reported that he had succeeded in raising queens by this method, and was accordingly reproved in an addendum to Keys' second book, published in 1796 while he lived in Bee Hall. This book was re-issued in 1814 under the title *A treatise on the breeding and management of bees.* It seems possible that Keys was a professional beekeeper who managed the bees of neighbouring gentry, for in the list of books he had read, several expensive and foreign books are recorded as having been presented to him by different gentlefolk.

Robert Sydserff

Our next author, Robert Sydserff, agreed with Butler that the queen's guards were distinguished by crests, tufts or tassels. Bees so marked can certainly be found at times in the hive, but they are not attendants of the queen, but foragers to whom the pollinia of a wild orchid have adhered. This is a good illustration of the need of combining two of the elements of scientific work : accurate observation, which was present here — and correct interpretation of the observation, which was lacking.

In his *Treatise on bees* Sydserff relates many stories of his adventures as a professional beekeeper engaged in helping his neighbours with their bees ; he was a great stickler for the truth as he knew it, but he leaves us amazed when he states his belief that the first sting hurts and causes swelling, and that later ones relieve the pain of the first and lessen the swelling.

Bryan J'Anson Bromwich

We have been considering for some time the activities of professional beekeepers, and their very apparent limitations ; it is now time to turn to *The experienced bee-keeper* who, from the title he gave to his book, might well have been another professional. He was, however, a clergyman ; he deserves special mention because his book attracted the notice of Dr. Coakley Lettsom and stirred him to write the pamphlet which led to the formation of the Western Apiarian Society. Bryan J'Anson Bromwich, the author, was an interesting writer. He was the first to discover the possibility of keeping more than one queen in a hive : three straw hives blew over in a high wind, and fell in such a position that the bees and their queens joined forces in one hive. As a result of this discovery, Bromwich experimented with collateral boxes ; he concluded that fertile queens will live together in amity, but that the presence of a single virgin causes fighting.

Bromwich was strongly opposed to sulphuring the bees, but like other writers of his time he does not seem to have realized that the development of a really satisfactory hive — in which bees could be deprived of their honey and yet kept through the winter — would have made the swarming problem much more urgent : the beekeeper would soon reach his maximum number of colonies, and what would then be done with surplus swarms ?

To return to the three queens : the idea of more than one queen in a hive seems to date back to Virgil, who spoke of two queens — a good and a bad — in the same hive. In the Middle Ages constant references are found to the danger of discouraging bees by giving over-large hives, and the knowledge of what happened when virgin queens emerged was ever present. This discovery by Bromwich may well have prompted the Wells hive (1896) and, although that particular hive was not a success, the idea of using multiqueen colonies has never since been allowed to die.

THE WESTERN APIARIAN SOCIETY

Bromwich believed that wax was formed from pollen, and he found an original way of justifying his idea — pointing out that little pollen was stored when wax was being produced. Like other writers on bees of this century, he designed a hive ; it was of no particular value, but his careful directions for extracting and caring for honey, for rendering wax and making mead, interested a famous physician, Dr. John Coakley Lettsom, who had a country house in Camberwell, and impelled him to write an essay entitled *Hints for promoting a Bee Society*. The second edition of this tract (1796) led to the formation of three Beekeeping Societies. One was called the Hamilton Beekeepers' Society ; of this nothing but the name seems to be known. The second, the British Apiarian Society, which was the child of Huish, got only so far as to print its rules. The third, however, the Western Apiarian Society (of Exeter) produced printed *Transactions* for about ten years from 1798 onwards, and its Secretary, the Reverend J. Isaac, published an admirable little book under the title of *The general apiarian*. A study of these *Transactions*, and of Isaac's book, gives a vivid picture of beekeeping as it was in the south-west at this time.

Meetings of the Society were held in a hotel in the Minster Yard (which was unfortunately destroyed during the Second World War), at times convenient to those who came to Exeter during the Sessions. The local gentry and nobility subscribed their guineas, which were used for paying premiums to cottagers who obtained heavy yields of honey without killing their bees.

It may be noted that the biggest ' take ' recorded by the Society was 146 pounds. Great care was taken to secure accuracy in weighing the honey taken from a hive which was entered for a premium, and overseers were appointed to superintend the operation of removing and weighing the honey.

The Secretary, who was the Unitarian Minister at Moretonhampstead, was the life and soul of the Society, and its papers were bright and interesting. The Society strongly favoured a hive in two parts, known as the Remunerator and the Preserver. The famous Scottish beekeeper, Bonner, sent a long letter for which he was awarded a premium, and a Mr. Allnutt stoutly defended his theory that queen bees were produced by immuring aged workers in queen cells.

At the height of all this activity the publication of the *Transactions** suddenly stopped, and the career of the Society came to an end. We do not know why ; the standard and interest of the last known volume of the *Transactions* was quite up to those of its predecessors. Another puzzle is why no further English Bee Society appeared until the eighteen-sixties were well advanced.

The records of the Western Apiarian Society remind the beekeeper of the existence of Thorley's son who had a shop called ' The Lock and Key ' opposite the Mansion House. There he sold the hives which his father had designed, and there he published the second edition of the *Melisselogia* in which he superseded his father's hive by one of his own invention, in which a great globe was placed above a skep in a manner somewhat reminiscent of the Remunerator and Preserver of the Western Apiarian Society.

SCIENTIFIC BOOKS AND TRANSLATIONS

It is the author's belief that whilst advances in practical beekeeping are dependent on the increase of scientific knowledge, and the increase of scientific knowledge is rendered possible or easier by improvements in methods of managing bees, the two rarely go hand in hand, but rather occupy the theatre of progress in turns. From 1650 until at least 1750 the main attention of intelligent English beekeepers was focused upon Mew's hive, White's collateral bee boxes and Wildman's hive with bars. Abroad, Réaumur and other scientists were making discoveries ; their works were read in this country, but the ruling impulse amongst intelligent and learned beekeepers seems to have been a desire to find some method whereby all members of the craft could collect their honey and wax without killing the bees.

By far the most important scientific work of the second half of the eighteenth century was the English translation of Swammerdam's *Biblia naturae*, which was published in 1758. Many copies are still

---

*The Secretary's own copy of the *Transactions* is at Dr. Williams' Library, Gordon Square, London.

in existence, and it must have been extensively read. It is a marvellous book ; the illustrations are so clear and accurate that they were reproduced in bee books until quite recently. The text is so good and contains so much original matter that the contents were not fully absorbed into the common stock of knowledge until the end of the century. An English summary of Maraldi's paper on bees had been published by Martyn and Chambers in 1742, and Bazin had issued an English translation of his *Histoire naturelle des abeilles* (which was a simple explanation of Réaumur's work) at the same time as the French edition (1744). Those Englishmen who were interested in bees were thus able to keep abreast of the discoveries which were being made by Réaumur and his circle. Unless they could read German, however, they could not become acquainted with the works of Schirach and Riem and of the Societies to which they belonged. The life and teachings of Anton Janscha were probably entirely unknown to them.

Arthur Murphy's poem entitled *The Bees* must be mentioned here. It was a poetical translation of a poem called *Praedium rusticum* which Vanière had published in 1730. Judged by the poetical standard of the time, Murphy's translation was both good and faithful, but it was quite out of date in bee knowledge when it was published (1799).

Papers in the Philosophical Transactions

The most famous English work of this period includes the paper on *Discoveries on the sex of bees* by John Debraw, read before the Royal Society on 21st November 1776, in which he stated his acquaintance with the work of Schirach, and of the Society of Kleinbautzen, confirmed by his own experiments the accuracy of Schirach's discovery, and propounded the theory that the drones fertilize the eggs of the queen in much the same way as in fishes, where the milter fertilizes the eggs of the spawner. He used glass hives, and observed that the drop of royal jelly which was beneath the egg was absorbed by it. He made a great point of the existence of drones of more than one size.

In a paper read on 22nd January 1778, Nathaniel Polhill, M.P., supported Debraw and stated his belief that, although the big drones were all killed at the end of the summer, the small drones were allowed to live through the winter, and fertilized the queen's eggs in the spring before the appearance of the large drones.

The much-quoted paper by the famous surgeon John Hunter, which was read to the Royal Society on 23rd February 1792, must now be mentioned. Hunter examined the bees himself, using thin hives made of plate glass in which windows were so contrived that he could readily reach any part of the comb. He was puzzled at the extensive geographical distribution of the honeybee, and found it hard to believe that it had been taken to America in a ship, because he noticed that his bees objected to their hives being kept closed. He stated that during severe weather bees retain their warmth by clustering, and that swarming bees always have full crops, which is not so with other bees. He rediscovered the dancing of bees which, so far as I know, had not been recorded since the time of Aristotle. His words were : ' We very often see some of the bees wagging their belly, as if tickled, running round, and to and fro, for only a little way, followed by one or two other bees as if examining them. I conceived that they were probably shaking out the cells of wax, and that the others were probably upon the watch to catch them '. Hunter also rediscovered [after Hornbostel, 1744] the true method of the formation of beeswax, and described very clearly how he found the wax scales and proved what they were. His paper is a model of careful work, and deserves the praise which has been given to it.

OTHER BOOKS

A scientific book of much less importance, but still interesting, is *Essays on the microscope* by George Adams, who was Mathematical Instrument Maker to King George III. The book is, more or less, a general history of insects ; it includes quotations from Swammerdam, Debraw and Schirach, but its most interesting features are a good illustration of a microscope of its date (1787), and another which shows the fold on the bee's wing which engages with the hooks on the other wing.

An anonymous book, which bears neither price nor date but which is stated to be sold by the booksellers of London and Westminster, is *The complete English, French and High German vermin killer*. This contains an article about bees, derived from classical sources but containing the suggestion that when hunting bees' nests, one should ' set sugared water and, when they come to sip, sprinkle some red, green or other colour upon them '.

Mention of classical beekeeping reminds us of the Reverend Thomas Owen who, about the turn of the century, published translations of Palladius and the *Geoponica*. They are fine, big volumes, which are useful today.

Another quasi-scientific book was *The virtues of honey* by Sir John Hill, a Covent Garden Apothecary. Although it was published in 1759, this work remained the only English treatise devoted solely to honey until the twentieth century had well begun. It deals with honey rather from the point of view of the seller, and describes the various kinds of fine foreign honey which Hill stocked, and the different types of British honey (the honey from East Hill, Wandsworth being especially good). A method of purifying honey is given, and its uses in medicine are considered. These are many : it is good for coughs, colds, asthma and stone. To obtain its full benefit the Syrup of Capillaire or the Aristaean Confection (both prepared by Hill) should be used. Hill's shop was in James Street, Covent Garden, but he lived in the country, where the Bayswater Tea Gardens were later established.

Several Scots books, one very famous (James Bonner's *New plan for speedily increasing the number of bee-hives in Scotland*) were published during this half century, but as the Scots came to the front as British beekeepers at the beginning of the nineteenth century, it will be convenient to deal with them together later on.

This account of the second half of the eighteenth century may conclude with the mention of a dainty little book of 140 pages entitled *A short history of bees in two parts* (1800). Part I deals with bees and their management, and is said to have been taken from later authors than Réaumur — amongst whom Swammerdam (1758) seems to be included. Part II is a sort of fairy story dealing with the pollination of plants. The book was evidently intended to be studied by young ladies in discreet schools, but a comparison with Gedde's or Warder's book makes it astonishingly clear that great advances in the knowledge of the bee had been made during the century.

CHAPTER VII

BEEKEEPING FROM 1800 TO 1850

THE ORDINARY BEEKEEPER

The opening of the nineteenth century may conveniently be regarded as a turning point in the history of beekeeping. Until 1800, science and practice in beekeeping had been considered completely distinct and unconnected. There were good reasons for this : the learned had been quite unsuccessful in their search for a hive which was fit to supersede the straw skep, and even as late as 1796 the skeppists were still occupied in replacing basket hives with skeps. In this year W. Pitt remarked in his *General view of the agriculture of the County of Stafford* (p. 154) : 'They succeed best in straw hives, neatly hooded over with an upper coating of straw'.

This fact is important because, although there were other (wooden) hives in existence, it was just as impossible to see what was happening in them as in the straw skeps. It is true that there were a few observation hives in the possession of scientists, but even in 1800 the ordinary practical beekeeper was unable to observe as much as the author of Book IX of Aristotle's *Natural History* had put on record.

These practical beekeepers were attracted by the writings of Robert Huish ; he possessed no scientific knowledge, but was an excellent skeppist, and gave good practical advice. He appeared to the skeppists as a man more likely to help them than the scientists, whose discoveries they found hard to believe and unrelated to their craft. Until his death in 1850, Huish continued to write in magazines, including monthly notes on beekeeping in the *Gardener, florist and apiculturist*, and a large following of beekeepers believed in him and his writings.

THE RISE OF ENTOMOLOGY

The years just before and after 1800 were marked by the appearance of a new phenomenon — the rise of entomology. Insects had been studied at least as early as the time of Moufet (1634)—indeed Aristotle wrote about them many centuries before — but bee scientists do not appear to have received much help from the entomologists until after the time of Huber.

The most famous of the early entomologists to be interested in bees was the Rev. W. Kirby who, in his *Monographia Apum Angliae* published

PLATE 7. Stewarton hive 'in full work', from Bartrum's *The Stewarton; the hive of the busy man* (1881); see pages 70 and 87.

in 1802, listed more than 300 species of native English bees, and recorded the eighteenth century English writers on entomology†. More influential than the *Monographia* was the *Introduction to entomology*, written by Kirby in collaboration with William Spence. The first volume of this book appeared in 1815 and the last in 1826 ; it is pleasantly written in the form of a series of letters, and rather reminds one of White's *Natural History of Selborne*. The Hubers are repeatedly quoted and their work accepted ; Huish received a good dressing down. Quite a good and interesting account of the hive bee is given ; the statement that combs are placed about half an inch apart, which is sufficient to allow two bees busied upon the opposite cells to pass each other with facility, is of interest because it foreshadowed Langstroth's discovery of the bee space.

SCOTTISH ENTOMOLOGISTS

In spite of the excellence of this work by Kirby and Spence, the Scots must be considered as the leading scientific beekeepers of this period.

The first English edition of Huber's works was published in Edinburgh anonymously in 1806, with a second edition in 1821. The translation, *New observations on the natural history of bees*, was made and published by two Scotsmen, Sir J. G. Dalyell and J. Anderson. It was not complete, but no other English translation appeared until C. P. Dadant's was published in 1926.

Sir William Jardine, who was partly responsible for the publication of Huber's work in Scotland, also edited the *Naturalist's Library*. The many volumes in this series included the excellent one on bees by the Rev. William Dunbar, Minister of Applegarth, published in 1840. This book was predominantly scientific, although it had a practical side. Its author had studied Huber, whose life is described in a Memoir at the beginning of the book and whose portrait appears as the frontispiece. Whether this study aroused Dunbar's interest in the scientific aspects of beekeeping we do not know, but in 1820 the *Edinburgh Philosophical Journal* published the first of a series of articles in which he described observations he had made by means of a single-frame hive, very similar to the observation hives in use at the present day. His drawing of bees engaged in wax making is hard to beat even now.

† BARBUT J. (1781) The genera insectorum of Linnaeus . . . *London : Sewell*
DONOVAN, EDWARD (1792) Natural history of British insects *London*
FORSTER, JOHN REINHOLD (1770) A catalogue of British insects *Warrington*
HARRIS, MOSES (1776) An exposition of English insects . . . *London : published by the author*
RAY, JOHN (1710) Historia insectorum *London*
SHAW, GEORGE The naturalist's miscellany . . . *London*
Philosophical Transactions
Transactions of the Linnean Society

One hundred and fifty pages of Dunbar's book were devoted to the bee itself, especially to the functions of queen, drone and worker, and various other questions which were engaging the attention of beekeepers at the time ; these included the mating of the queen and the raising of queens from worker eggs. The next eighty pages dealt with the practical management of bees and included twenty in which various forms of hives were described. The final forty pages gave some idea of bumble bees and ' foreign bees ' (honeybees and others), which had not been dealt with since Purchas published his *Theatre of politicall flying-insects* in 1657.

The importance of the work which was done by people in Scotland about the year 1820 is not generally recognized, and more research is needed to reveal its full extent. The following were amongst the papers which appeared in the *Edinburgh Philosophical Journal* in 1820-1821 : Dunbar's accounts of his ' glazed bee-hive', and of his observations on the introduction of two queens into this hive; the Reverend Andrew Jameson's letter about wooden hives ; Sir George Mackenzie's letter on the vision of the humble bee and the honeybee ; Dr. Dunbar's observations on the conversion of worker larvae into queens.

In the final years of the eighteenth century and the beginning of the nineteenth, James Bonner was at the height of his fame. His *Bee-masters' companion* was published in Berwick-on-Tweed in 1789 and *A new plan for speedily increasing the number of bee-hives in Scotland* in Edinburgh in 1795. Extracts from a letter of his, and an article for which he was awarded a premium, appeared in the transactions of the Western Apiarian Society.

To this list of Scots beekeeping authors and authorities, with whom England had few to compare, must be added the names of two very remarkable men.   Dr. J. N. Tennent (1951) drew attention to a book written by the Reverend James Playfair, who died in 1812.   The book, which was never published, was entitled *Of the care and knowledge of bees*, and describes the observations and discoveries of the author who, working alone and with a comparatively small microscope, had rediscovered many of Réaumur's results. It was a remarkable manuscript, which also contained advice about practical beekeeping and a description of a hive invented by the author.

One other author is equally noteworthy.   In 1822 and 1834 two tiny editions of a book entitled *Rara liber* [sic] were produced by a certain Raoul or Robert Russell, about whom we know only that he lived in Elgin. The writer seems to have read all the bee books which were then current, and the facts contained in his work are well judged and carefully selected. The most remarkable feature about the book, however, is its making. The author found about a hundred old pieces of type ; he cut out more by hand as required, set the type, printed the book, made the plates for the illustrations, and finally bound it himself. It is an interesting example of Scottish energy and self-reliance.

ENGLISH BOOKS ON BEES AND BEEKEEPING

The most famous English author of this period was Dr. Bevan. His portrait, prefixed to a memoir in Volume II of *The Naturalist* (1838), shows a chubby little man, remarkably like Mr. Pickwick. The first edition of his *Honey-bee* appeared in 1827 ; the second (dedicated by permission to Queen Victoria) in 1838. A third edition, much revised by Bevan's old friend W. A. Munn, appeared in 1870. This book was far better known than Dunbar's, whom it often quotes ; it was well up to date and covered a very wide range of subjects connected with bees and bee-keeping. Foreign hives were described, and also enemies of bees, some foreign bees and other subjects. The general interest of this book, combined with the sound views it presented and the advocacy of skeps of improved patterns, made it widely acceptable. The book was entirely suited to its time, and remained the standard English work on bees for almost as long a period as Butler's *Feminine monarchie*.

Dr. Bevan resembled Charles Butler in another way. Butler's book was a great improvement on all that had gone before, but he remained faithful to skeps. So to a great extent did Bevan, and he — like Butler — was followed by an advocate of wooden hives. This was Thomas Nutt who in 1832 (at Wisbech) published *Humanity to honey bees*, in which he described his collateral hives. These were a revival of the hives of the Reverend Stephen White, but with some slight modifications. In spite of the author's confession that he had never read a bee book, and the fact that 155 out of the 269 pages were devoted to hives, the book was very successful. This was due to its attractive title, and to its rejection of the skeppist's practice of sulphuring bees. A large number of Nutt's hives were sold, and a few are still in existence. However they did not — as was hoped — eliminate swarming, nor produce great quantities of honey. In the course of a few years they were superseded by other types.

The last attempt to revive the collateral system was made in 1843, when John Jones of Hereford published a book called *The eclectic hive*, describing his ' Herefordshire collateral bee boxes '. This author must not be confused with T. R. Jones, Professor of Anatomy at King's College, London, who in 1845 published a *Natural History of animals* which included 41 pages on Hymenoptera. This was a useful popular scientific work, which enabled beekeepers to understand the position of their bees in the insect world.

SCOTTISH BEEKEEPERS

Scotland, which had given a lead in the science of beekeeping, had also come to the fore in beekeeping practice. Before Nutt revived the idea of a collateral hive, Robin Ker or Kerr of Stewarton in Ayrshire had become famous in Scotland for his ' Stewarton ' hive (1819), which was an improved form of Gedde's supered hive, and made of thicker timber. It was a very good hive, and an adaptable one. Unfortunately Ker wrote no book, and the hive did not spread much beyond Galloway. However some Stewarton hives fitted with frames were in use until the end of the century; see Plate 7 (page 66). A detailed history of the hive is given by Struthers (1951).

Another Scot, Dr. James Hewison, read an interesting paper about bees to the Caledonian Horticultural Society on 13th December 1814. However the one who came nearest to rivalling Dr. Bevan was T. M. Howatson, whose book *The apiarian's manual* also appeared in 1827. Howatson invented a good, practical bar hive which had upper and lower entrances, and a float feeder of an original design. He was well read and gave a good summary of bee anatomy, derived from authors who had themselves studied the subject. He seems to have studied all the available bee books, including those by Huber and Keys, and he describes practically all the hives then in existence, including the Favignana hive, and Wheler's and Huish's.

A translation of the work of the Swiss pastor Jonas de Gélieu, by Miss Stirling Graham, was published anonymously in Edinburgh in 1829, under the title *The bee preserver*. This book was well known in England and, like Nutt's book, is noteworthy in that it shows the importance and strength of the movement to eliminate the practice of sulphuring bees.

A link between English and Scottish beekeeping is provided by James Rennie, an Aberdonian who was Professor of Natural History in King's College, London, from 1830 to 1834. Amongst the three books which he wrote for the Library of Entertaining Knowledge, the one entitled *Insect architecture* (1830) dealt mainly with bees and wasps.

BEEKEEPING APPLIANCE MAKERS

Some of the beekeeping books published in the first half of the nineteenth century were mainly intended to publicize new types of hive, and a few were the products of what was almost a new profession — the making of beekeeping appliances. In the previous two centuries Gedde, Worlidge, Warder, Thorley and Stephen White had sold (or recommended) their own hives only. The two Wildmans, Thomas and Daniel, had sold hives of several types, but they could hardly be called professional appliance makers, inasmuch as their income appears to have come chiefly from attending to other people's bees.

John Milton

John Milton was a professed appliance merchant. His first work, *The London apiarian guide*, was published in London in 1823, from the

Apiarian Repository at 175 Strand. (Milton afterwards traded at the Italian and Bee Warehouse, 10 Marylebone Street, Wimpole Street.) Of the 21 pages of this little book 14 are devoted to what Milton designated as his newly invented double-topped straw hive, the double cottage straw hive, a superior box hive, the hexagon box hive and straw hive (with slider and grating for working a large glass hive on the top) and the common hive. The rest of the book deals with purchasing bees, bee flowers, swarming, hiving, uniting, feeding, the feeding machine, and honey. It was little more than a catalogue in book form.

The next edition (1843) was called *The practical beekeeper* ; it contained about 150 pages, and was a much more serious work. It contains descriptions of many more hives, and of other appliances which Milton sold ; the greater part of the book was almost certainly written by W. C. Cotton, and likewise the invaluable ' List of Books and Writers upon the Bee '. From Cotton's writings we are aware that he knew Milton, and we also know that Cotton sailed to New Zealand after he had published *My bee book* in 1842.

The third edition of Milton's book of 1851 was less pretentious. The beekeeping matter of the first edition was reinstated but rearranged, and still more hives were described. On the other hand Cotton's notes and the List of books and writers on bees had disappeared ; the reason is not known.

George and Alfred Neighbour

George Neighbour established his business in Holborn about 1814, not very far from Daniel Wildman's shop ; it was moved to 149 Regent Street in 1852. Alfred Neighbour, his more famous son, was born in Holborn in 1825.

Neighbour and Milton exhibited bee appliances side by side at the Great Exhibition of 1851, and both published pictures of their stands. Alfred Neighbour is remembered because he and Woodbury received Italian queens from Hermann of Switzerland at the same time (1859). The first edition of his book *The apiary* was published in 1865.

Alfred Neighbour purchased Tegetmeier's library of bee books which was sold to Colonel H. J. O. Walker when Neighbour died in 1890 ; Colonel Walker finally sold it to the University of Wisconsin in 1930, where it became the nucleus of the Miller Memorial Library.

WILLIAM CHARLES COTTON

The Reverend William Charles Cotton may possibly have been descended from Charles Cotton, part author of Walton's *Compleat angler*. His family was certainly a notable one, for his great grandfather, grandfather, father and brother, and William Charles himself, are all mentioned in the *Dictionary of National Biography*. Whilst he was still an undergraduate at Christ Church, Oxford, he founded the Oxford Apiarian Society, and published and republished his *Short and simple letter to cottagers* (1837). This was followed in 1842 by *My bee book*. Good, sound advice for bee-keepers of the period is given here; intermingled with it is a miscellaneous selection of articles of interest about bees and beekeeping, culled from many sources, old and new, English and foreign. The production of this delightful miscellany seems to have been prompted by a pure love of bees. Cotton never published a second edition, perhaps because Milton had used the materials which he had collected.

When Cotton went to New Zealand in 1842 he took his bees with him; they were almost the first bees to reach the country. He soon published *A manual for New Zealand beekeepers* at Wellington (1848). In 1872, after he had returned to England and was Rector of Frodsham, near Chester, he published under the title *Buzz a buzz* a translation of a humorous German book about bees, called *Schnurrdiburr*, by Wilhelm Busch. When Cotton died in 1879 he left his bee books to the Rectory, and they so filled the study that his successors could not use it. The collection is at present on loan to the Library of the Ministry of Agriculture; in addition to rare early English books, it contains more early German bee books than any other library in London.

THE TRANSITION FROM SKEPS TO MOVABLE-FRAME HIVES

In the year of publication of *My bee book* (1842) the *Quarterly Review* contained an article on ' The honey-bee ' by the Reverend Thomas James. This article was later republished as a small book, and was much read. It contains a readable account of beekeeping in classical times, and a general discussion on beekeeping in England with quotations from writers of previous centuries and of his own time. James' preference for skeps, whether of the early simpler kind or adorned with glasses, is evident, but he also described hives of all types, new and old, and aroused interest in them. He was probably right in preferring skeps to the fixed-comb hive then in existence, but progress towards the movable-comb hive continued throughout the decade.

William Augustus Munn, who was another friend of Bevan's and edited the third edition of his book in 1870, published a book of his own in 1844 : *A description of the bar- and frame-hive*, which he had invented. Although clumsy, this hive was workable. The illustration of it in Bevan's third edition (1870) is not nearly so clear as those which appeared in the *Gardener's Chronicle* for 1843 and Munn's own *Description*. Although it is clear from the illustration that the frames could certainly be removed from the hive, they seem to have been adapted from Huber's leaf hive, and do not appear to foreshadow Langstroth's invention in any way.

NEVER KILL A BEE

The writers on practical beekeeping which remain to be dealt with can be divided into two classes : those who were impressed with the cruelty of killing the bees when taking their honey in the autumn — and who were therefore advocates of new methods and newly invented hives — and those who desired to make the best of the old ways.

George Strutt was the first of these ' humanitarian ' writers. In his book *The practical apiarian, or a treatise on the improved management of bees*, which was published at Clare in Suffolk in 1825, he writes as a professional beekeeper, and boasts of having taken 84 pounds of honey, and a cast and a swarm, from one hive in the same year. His hives were boxes, apparently octagonal, which he had invented in 1822, and which he kept on benches in bee houses. He strongly disapproved of sulphuring bees, and of straw hives of every type ; his book is still quite readable, and contains hints which can be useful even now.

The apiarian's guide by J. H. Payne, which was published in 1833, is an enlarged edition of his *Cottager's guide* which had appeared in 1832. The book was written to induce beekeepers to use the improved cottage hive, a flat-topped skep with a hole in the top, on which boxes could be placed ; as these could be removed when they were full, the practice of sulphuring the bees was dispensed with. The last chapter of this book describes Nutt's hive, which had just appeared. It deserves careful study by anyone who wishes to understand the mind of the intelligent beekeeper at this date. Swammerdam, Réaumur, de Gélieu and Bevan are all mentioned and approved — but so also is Huish who, as a practical beekeeper, is singled out for approbation. The author, however, kept quite clear of the Huber-Huish controversy, and it is evident that he thought more of Nutt than of anyone else.

Bees were traditionally placed near the house, and as the men were often out and the women at home, it seems reasonable to suppose that the women commonly looked after the bees as well as the fowls. The first author to write especially for women beekeepers was Samuel Bagster, whose *Management of bees* contained a description of his " ladies' safety hive ". Another novel feature of this book was the coloured frontispiece ; this shows the queen, worker and drone, both life-size and magnified. The drawing of the queen is specially interesting, because it shows clearly what may be called the ' square shoulder ' of the abdomen, which seems to have characterized the old British bee. The book is largely a compilation, but the author describes several of the hives in current use ; his own ladies' hive seems more complicated than any other known hive. Bagster was a great believer in hive ventilation, as was Nutt, and they seem to have been the first to write upon the subject.

The best known beekeeping book of this period (apart from those by Bevan and Nutt) was *The beekeeper's manual* by Henry Taylor, which was first published in 1838; in some ways this book has a modern flavour.

It begins with a short account of the queen, worker and drone (the only scientific material in the book), but the author carefully avoids any reference to the Huber controversy. A great deal of space is devoted to descriptions of the various kinds of hives which were known to the author ; he begins with the ordinary skep and its later developments — skeps with supers and with wooden bars. Then wooden hives are described, especially those with bars, and White's and Nutt's collateral hives — of these he has no great opinion. (Many thinking beekeepers of this period seem to have concluded that if skeps were to be discarded and the sulphuring of bees abandoned, a hive must be produced which would allow the removal of surplus honey without damaging the brood nest.) A short chapter upon bee pasturage follows ; this was a new idea in bee books. Finally there were the four long chapters which give the book its modern appearance : summer management, autumn management, winter management and spring management.

The popularity of the collateral hive at this time is shown by the publication in 1843 of *The eclectic hive* by John Jones of Hereford.

Matthew Pile of Gateshead also believed in the collateral system, which he applied to straw skeps. His *Bee cultivator's assistant* (1838) again shows the urge which, in the days before Langstroth, was driving progressive beekeepers to seek a type of hive which would enable them to obtain more honey and to avoid killing their bees ; it also exemplifies the readiness with which people who knew little of beekeeping — but thought they had discovered a short cut to perfection — rushed into print. Pile devised a wooden hive, which he termed the ' Mellifluous or Perpetual Motion Hive '. Some of his ideas were incorrect, but the monthly calendar at the end of his book was by far the longest and most comprehensive which had appeared.

OTHER BOOKS ABOUT BEES

In *The cottager's bee-book* (1839) Richard Smith objected strongly to the ' Never kill a bee ' principle, and attacked the ' Conservative beekeeper ', who recommended ' conserving ' the bees instead of killing them. It must be remembered that those people who encouraged swarms were likely to regard old colonies of bees as a nuisance, and best destroyed.

In spite of its low price, Robert Golding's *Shilling bee book* (1847) was the work of a first-class beekeeper who had helped in the preparation of Bevan's *Honey bee*. It contained a great deal of up-to-date information, and was a dangerous rival to Huish's book, which was much dearer.

In 1818 John Lawrence, who adopted the pseudonym of Bonington Moubray, published *A practical treatise . . . on breeding all kinds of domestic poultry*. To the fourth edition (1822) he added a section about bees ; it was a compilation from other authors. He stated that he took no interest in bees until 1787 ; at that time honey was being sold at 2d. a pound in

Hampshire and Essex, whereas at the time of publication higglers were buying it for 6d. a pound, and wax at about 18 or 20 pence. At these prices the author considered beekeeping to be profitable. He believed that the part of Essex near Braintree and Bocking produced some of the finest honey in England. Though the author was a follower of Huish, he was a good East Anglian and would have nothing to do with ' single stools ' : ' Hives either stand in a bee-house, box or shed, or under a thatched or some kind of roof.'

The farmer's encyclopaedia by C. W. Johnston, F.R.S., contains articles on the bee-eater, honey and wax. At that date (1842) the bee-eater seems to have nested regularly in Norfolk. The use of the smoke of puff-balls or tobacco is recommended when manipulating.

In 1829 Mrs. Christian Isobel Johnstone published, in her *Scenes of industry*, a most affecting account of the misfortune which overtook Letitia Welbeck, when out walking in a crocodile from her school ; she stepped on a bee's nest and had to be carried home. One result of this occurrence was that the young ladies were taken at regular intervals to a nearby apiary to learn beekeeping; in the book Letitia asks the beekeeper many questions, which are so arranged that they give openings for long and instructive replies.

The last two books to be mentioned provide an interesting link with Poland. In *The history and management of bees*, John Wighton described the ' improved Polish hive ', a picture of which forms the frontispiece of the book (1842) ; it is simply a hive cut out of an upright tree trunk. The book contains quotations from Dunbar, Cotton, Huish, Payne and Nutt ; it has occasional out-of-the-way information about bees in Cuba, Livonia, Russia and Poland. In general it may be said that the author disbelieved all statements which he could not confirm ; he said that bees were of no use in apple orchards because apples were wind pollinated, and he also disbelieved in the power of the workers to lay drone eggs. He did however manage to confirm a surprisingly large number of the recent new discoveries.

In 1845 the real Polish hive was described for the benefit of English readers by Dobrogost Chylinski in his *Bee-keeper's manual*. It was a hollow log 3½ to 5 feet high, with a diameter tapering from 20 inches at the base to 8 inches at the top. There was no base, but the roof was covered with a large clay pan ; the top half of the hive was bound with cord. This hive closely resembled Wighton's, and was the precursor of the foreign appliances which had so marked an effect on English beekeeping in the next half-century.

CONCLUSION

The first half of the nineteenth century might well be described as a time of frustration. Except in Scotland, where the Stewarton hive was in local use but comparatively neglected elsewhere, there was much doing but little done. The scientists made no very wonderful discoveries — perhaps partly because no improvements in practical beekeeping had turned their thoughts into new channels. The practical beekeepers were still unable to discover how to make a frame hive, although the question had been puzzling them and their forebears for two hundred years — ever since the days of Gedde and Plot. There were great events to come, but they did not start until the first year of the next half-century.

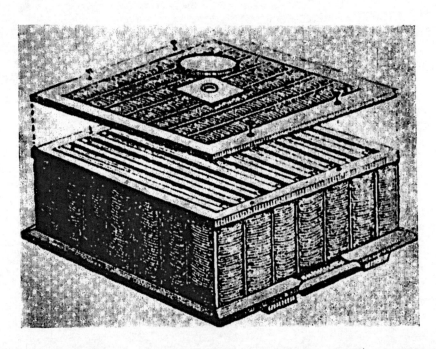

PLATE 8. Brood chamber of the Woodbury hive, first made in 1862 (see page 85), from Neighbour's *The apiary* (1865). Woodbury introduced Langstroth's movable-comb beekeeping into England.

CHAPTER VIII

BEEKEEPING FROM 1850 TO 1900

BEEKEEPING INVENTIONS

In 1851 the great discovery for which the beekeeping world had been striving for three centuries was at last made : in the United States Langstroth showed how to make a frame which could be removed from the hive at will, since the bees would not attach it to the hive walls. The results of this discovery were not in evidence immediately, and even now many fixed-comb hives can be found : indeed if the Langstroth frame had stood alone, it might conceivably have remained the toy of the wealthy and a special instrument of scientists. However its invention was followed by a number of others (which were initiated by it), and it was their combined effect which revolutionized beekeeping and made it so vastly superior to that of the previous ages.

There were five of these inventions, although some of them were developments of old ideas rather than completely new inventions ; all were necessary if the full advantage of the movable-comb hives was to be obtained. They were : wax foundation, the queen excluder, the centrifugal extractor, the smoker, and the bee escape. The following dates are those given by Mr. Frank Pellett in his *History of American beekeeping* ; for inventions which were developed gradually the date he gives is that of the preliminary attempt and not of the complete solution to the problem.

The first and most important supplement to the Langstroth frame was wax foundation, the invention of which is credited to Johannes Mehring (Germany) in 1857 ; his work was perfected by E. B. Weed (U.S.A.), who in 1891 taught the Americans how to make foundation on a commercial scale, and by Captain J. E. Hetherington (U.S.A.) who succeeded in supporting the foundation with wires.

The year 1865 saw two further inventions. In France the Abbé Collin perfected the queen excluder and so enabled beekeepers to guarantee that honey from movable-frame hives would be free from brood, brood food, *etc.* In 1865 Major Hruschka, an Austrian, devised the centrifugal honey extractor, which made it possible to collect this honey without destroying the combs.

Smokers had been in use for many centuries — the Egyptians certainly used them — but the advent of the movable frame made a new type

of smoker necessary.   It was no longer desirable to produce a great torrent
of smoke to drive the bees out of the hive along with their queen ; what was
required was a comparatively gentle cloud of smoke to subdue the bees but
not alarm them excessively.   Many attempts to attain this end were made,
and it is difficult to say exactly who should be credited with the invention ;
T. F. Bingham (U.S.A.) seems to have the best claim, in 1877.

When these inventions had been perfected, the beekeeper was able to
supply pure, clean honey to his customers ; however the difficulty of removing the honey from a hive full of bees remained.   This was overcome in
1891 when E. C. Porter (U.S.A.) began to sell his bee escape, which made
it possible for the beekeeper to prevent the bees from returning to his
supers, and thus to remove the honey without any risk of being stung, or
of damaging the bees.

This story of progressive improvements in beekeeping appears to be
so natural and inevitable that one is tempted to assume that all beekeepers accepted the devices as they came out.   This was far from being the
case : even now some skeps are in use in England, and in many other
countries, and box hives in the United States.   Two sound reasons can be
given for this.   Firstly skeps and boxes are cheap ; secondly skep or box
beekeeping is the easiest way of keeping bees, and the comparative small-
ness of the yield of honey is to some extent compensated for in poor
districts by the relative certainty of the yield.

Bearing in mind the high cost of frames, the time used in nailing them
together and in inserting the wax foundation, whether wired or unwired,
it can reasonably be stated that the frame hive owes its success to two
factors : the purity of the honey obtained by its use, and its ability to yield
large quantities of honey in good districts.   Its weakness is that relatively
large quantities of wax foundation and wood are required and, if a time
should come when these are not available cheaply, beekeepers may well
find it necessary to make considerable changes in their methods.

GENERAL DEVELOPMENTS

This multifold progress makes the history of British beekeeping from
the year 1850 onwards more and more difficult to describe.   Many
influences combine to make it hard to disentangle the various lines along
which progress was being made.   The great and growing influence of
America has already been made clear, and other countries also played their
part in the progress of British beekeeping.

The history of bee anatomy is doubly involved : not only were
researches carried out in many countries, but they were frequently the
work of entomologists who had no interest in beekeeping, and did not
publish their results in papers which were read by beekeepers.

As in the previous half-century, the writers on practical beekeeping in
Britain were at first divided into those who wrote and made their systems

to suit hives of their own invention, and those who tried to embody in their publications the methods which were in accordance with the new ideas then appearing. These new ideas made beekeepers more aware of, and on the look-out for, further improvements; this, in turn, led to a desire for intercommunication, which was expressed by the foundation of the *British Bee Journal* in 1873 and of the British Bee-Keepers' Association in 1874. For some years this body did a great deal to help beekeepers, and the papers read at its meetings and the books it produced did much to raise the status of the craft. After a time it was realized that one central body could not give the personal assistance which beginners and others required, and this led to the formation, first of local Associations, and by 1876 of county Associations, to encourage co-operation between the local branches.

After the foundation of the British Bee-Keepers' Association, and especially after the standardization of the brood frame and shallow frame in 1882, the two types of author mentioned above gradually drew together, and an excellent system of beekeeping was evolved; however, this was then elaborated until it comprised so many details that it lost its flexibility, and thereby its pre-eminence. Within this half-century the twentieth-century methods of management, which have now partly taken its place, began to make their appearance; they were based on the methods adopted by American and English commercial beekeepers and have been very successful in many areas. However they can never obtain universal acceptance, since they are based on the assumption that those who use them have apiaries situated in highly productive honey districts.

During this period a small number of what may be called literary bee books were published. These books, which are somewhat rare in all languages, are on the whole unusually attractive and do more than any other type of book to interest outsiders in our subject.

One feature of beekeeping in the twentieth century has been the emergence of specialization. Besides the professional beekeepers who aim at obtaining honey for sale, there are beekeepers who rear queens, those who sell bees, and those who rent out their bees for pollination purposes. Along with this specialization, there has naturally been an emergence of books devoted to a special part of beekeeping. These books began to appear before 1900, but they were few in number and dealt mainly with queen rearing.

BOOKS DEALING WITH BEE ANATOMY

Experience seems to show that, in the past at all events, improvements in practical beekeeping and advances in knowledge were rarely contemporary. We should therefore not necessarily expect the very great improvements in the methods of keeping bees, which were developed in the second half of the nineteenth century, to be accompanied by a

F

special interest in the anatomy of the bee. The interesting point in the science of the present period is the extent to which it was in fact influenced by the advances in practical work. The attempts at bee breeding could hardly have been feasible before the advent of the movable frame. Bee diseases had been known since ancient times, but the movable frame at last made it possible to study them in more detail — and probably also helped to spread them. The movable frame paved the way for an adequate understanding of the behaviour of bees in the colony, which is necessary as a basis for any modern method of management.

A great discovery (parthenogenesis) was made on the Continent just before 1850 ; this was assimilated and accepted in England during the decade 1850–1860, with the result that a first-class book on the anatomy of the honeybee was published in 1860 by James Samuelson and J. Braxton Hicks. A period of apparent quiescence followed ; no books on bee anatomy were published, but individual students were studying separate organs of the bee and of other insects, and they published their results in the journals of the Societies to which they happened to belong — the Royal Microscopical Society, the Quekett Microscopical Club, the Entomological Society, and others. Each new writer about bee anatomy — or indeed about any aspect of bee culture — therefore had to have a much more extensive knowledge than had been necessary earlier. It was no longer sufficient for him to know the current bee literature and to be in touch with a few leading scientists ; he must have sufficient scientific training to enable him to read papers in various scientific journals and to appraise their value. In order to collect and register the discoveries contained in these papers, he must have access to a good library. Finally, when all the available information — new and old — had been collected, he must fuse it into a connected whole. It is not surprising, therefore, that it was not until the last decade of the century that another book on bee anatomy appeared.

The important discovery of parthenogenesis, referred to above, was described by Johann Dzierzon in 1848 in his *Theorie und Praxis des neuen Bienenfreundes*. The facts of parthenogenesis had been known in part to Hunter, Riem and Schirach, but Dzierzon originated the theory which explained it as it occurs in the bee. Parthenogenesis in alternate generations as it is found in the aphids was already known, and it had been thought that parthenogenesis in bees was explicable in the same manner. The whole subject was examined by Professor Carl Theodor Ernst von Siebold, whose book was translated by W. S. Dallas and published in London in 1857 : *On a true parthenogenesis in moths and bees*. This book made clear the different kinds of parthenogenesis to be found in different insects. No English edition of Dzierzon's book appeared until 1882, when a translation of the 1878 edition, entitled *Rationelle Bienenzucht*, was published under the aegis of C. N. Abbott (founder of the *British Bee Journal* and the British Bee-Keepers' Association). In 1867, however, John Lowe read to the Entomological Society a paper in which he stated that when a virgin queen of pure race mates with a drone of another race, a proportion of the drone progeny is affected by the mating. It is a pity that this question was lost sight of, for investigations which proved the incorrectness of Lowe's statements would probably, in so doing, have given some idea of what is meant by the purity of the queen's lineage, and might even have led to the discovery of 'multiple mating' in the nineteenth century.

In 1860 James Samuelson and Dr. J. Braxton Hicks, whom the author can just remember from his childhood, as Coroner for South-West London, combined to produce *The honey-bee* which, like Siebold's book, was published in London by J. van Voorst. This book contains eight plates only, but the illustrations on them were chosen with skill and care, and as many as possible were placed on each plate. It is an octavo book of about 160 pages, 116 of which are devoted to the bee, and the remainder to the psychology of insects. It is in principle an outline of the anatomy of the bee ; it is written in a systematic manner, and shows great skill in covering much ground in a small compass.

F. R. Cheshire was the author of the next book on bee anatomy. He was a schoolmaster who began to keep bees in 1871. In 1873 he published his *Practical bee-keeping* which will be mentioned later. He was a member of the Royal Microscopical Society, and his work in conjunction with Dr. W. Watson Cheyne culminated in a paper which was read to the Society on 11th March 1885, in which the discovery of *Bacillus alvei* was reported, and declared to be the cause of foul brood.

In the next year Cheshire published the first volume of his *Bees and bee-keeping*, which remained the standard English textbook for at least forty years. This volume dealt with the anatomy of the bee and the pollination of flowers. Some of the illustrations resembled the large diagrams which the British Bee-Keepers' Association had previously published for the author. So far as the writer knows, the whole work was far in advance of any previous book, British or foreign, both in matter and arrangement. The second volume, which was published in 1888, dealt with practical beekeeping and was a most useful handbook in its day. It is difficult at the time of writing to appraise its real value, and it — like Cowan's *British bee-keeper's guide book* — seems to have reached the time when it is least valued. Several causes have contributed to this : firstly, it has long been the fashion among some to decry British farming methods and regard American practice as suitable for use in all parts of this country ; secondly, the native bee has completely or almost completely disappeared, through acarine disease, and has been replaced by more prolific races which require

somewhat different treatment ; lastly, it has perhaps not been fully understood that Cheshire's book was really addressed to members of the middle
class who kept bees in their spare time.

Dr. T. W. Cowan published his small book on the anatomy of the
bee in 1890. This and his *British bee-keeper's guide book*, which first
appeared in 1881, were far in advance of any books except Cheshire's ; even
today they are models of system, conciseness and comprehensiveness. *The
honey bee* contains at least one statement which is now known to be quite
incorrect (that the brood is fed on regurgitated food); this does not alter
the fact that the book was singularly well adapted for its time.

OTHER SCIENTIFIC BOOKS

A few books should now be mentioned which, although they do not
primarily deal with beekeeping, are nevertheless of interest to beekeepers.

The first of these, *British bees* by W. E. Shuckard, was published in
1866 and is described on the title page as ' An introduction to the study of
the natural history and economy of the bees indigenous to the British
Isles '. The work has been done well, and the coloured plates at the end of
the volume are beautifully executed and make the identification of the bees
portrayed quite easy. This was almost the first of many books which have
enabled beekeepers of the present century to take an interest in the natural
history of bees in general, and in the flowers and fruit they pollinate.

Other famous works of interest to beekeepers are : *Ants, bees and
wasps* by Sir John Lubbock (Lord Avebury) in 1882, *The senses, instincts
and intelligence of animals* by the same author, and *Animal intelligence*
by Georges Romanes in 1882. All contain references to bees.

The *British Bee Journal*, which began as a monthly but developed into
a weekly paper (becoming fortnightly in 1956), has been published con-
tinuously since 1874 ; until 1900 it was the only beekeeping periodical
published in Britain. It worked in close conjunction with the British Bee-
Keepers' Association, which between the years 1880 and 1900 did a great
deal of good by the pamphlets it published on the scientific aspects of
beekeeping, and by the powerful influence it exerted to promote every
aspect of progress in beekeeping, both theoretical and practical.

NEW SYSTEM OF MANAGEMENT

A number of beekeepers appeared on the scene who invented new
systems of management which were very popular for a time, but which
failed to establish themselves permanently. The first of these was J. W.
Pagden of Alfriston, in Sussex, who in 1868 published a book entitled
£70 a year ; how I make it by my bees. In those happy days a cottager
who made £70 a year considered that he was doing well, and Pagden wished
other people to follow his example. He believed in cheap hives and used
skeps : those who did otherwise were ' people of a Scientific, Poetical and

Searching Mind '. In the winter, inverted American cheese boxes were placed on four bricks, and on these boxes stood the skeps—protected by old sacks topped by milk pans. All the honey was taken, and sugar syrup was fed to the bees ; this was not a bad plan with skep beekeeping. Pagden's method of checking swarming, which he claimed to have invented, was the placing of a swarm on the old stand. He removed his honey from the supers (boxes placed above a hole in the top of the skep) by removing them, bees and all, and covering them with a box in which were a number of holes stopped with corks. A cork was removed to allow the bees out ; when some tried to return, that cork was replaced and another removed. This was continued until no bees remained.

Alfred Rusbridge published his *Bee-keeping plain and practical and how to make it pay* in 1883. He lived at Sidlesham, near Chichester. Besides his apiary, he owned a hive works, and he was a regular contributor to the early numbers of the *British Bee Journal*. He recommended his own hives ; he remarked that from one of his hives a bell glass of white clover honey was removed which fetched 5/- a pound at the Crystal Palace. In his opinion bees kept in a bee-house were likely to be quite a fortnight in advance of those kept outside. The best site for an apiary was in the form of an oval, with the hives facing inwards and surrounded by a hedge of laurustinus or of flowering currant. Like most successful beekeepers, Rusbridge lived in a good district.

BEE BOOKS FOR DIFFERENT COUNTRIES

The first place in this division belongs by right to the American *ABC of bee culture*, which was originally published by A. I. Root in December 1877. This is now the oldest of ' living ' bee books, that is, the oldest book which is still being revised and brought up to date.

The book which for long excelled the *ABC* in point of years was also of American origin : Langstroth's *The hive and honey-bee*. It was bound to happen that successive editions of this book contained less and less of what Langstroth had written, and it was eventually replaced by a worthy successor bearing the same title.

A new type of specialized bee book had been begun by Cotton in 1848 when he published his *Manual for New Zealand beekeepers*. This was followed in 1881 by *The illustrated New Zealand bee manual*, which was written by the Colony's Apiarist, Isaac Hopkins. Hopkins subsequently migrated to Australia, and published *The illustrated Australasian bee manual* in 1886. Meanwhile John Douglas had stirred up the Government of India, and made them publish *A collection of papers on bee-keeping in India* in 1883, which he followed up in 1884 with *A hand-book of bee-keeping for India*, and a paper which he read to the Asiatic Society in 1886 in which he suggested that India was the original home of the hive bee.

Canada had shared in the beekeeping experiences of the United States, and South Africa completed the tale of the British Dominions when, in 1890, Henry L. Attridge (Lecturer on Agriculture in the South African Agricultural College) published his *South African bees and their practical management in movable-comb hives*, which was republished in Dutch and English in 1909.

With this mention of the commencement of bee literature in the Dominions, we must also remember the outlying parts of the British Isles. In 1888 the first Welsh bee book *Y gwenynydd* (The beekeeper) was published at Bala. The authors were H. P. Jones and D. Michael and, to judge from the available descriptions of it, the authors did their best to produce a book which would be a credit to their land.

In 1895 a very small (6d.) book on beekeeping was published in Dublin ; it was written by J. M. Gillies and entitled *Stepping-stones to bee-keeping*.

The use of fungus for stupefying bees during manipulations was revived and strongly advocated in *The bee and bee-keeper's friend* by Mrs. J. B. Pratt, which was published in Aberdeen in 1853. Another book, *The management of bees* by Dr. John Mackenzie, appeared in Edinburgh and London in 1860. At this time the great band of earlier Scottish writers had passed away, and their successors had not yet appeared.

THE FIRST IMPORTS OF ITALIAN BEES

While the Dominions were engaged in organizing beekeeping in their own territories, a new enterprise of the first importance was engaging the attention of beekeepers in England and the U.S.A. If a beekeeper visits French Switzerland he will find beekeepers there using what are commonly known as Italian queens but, if he enquires from whence they are bought, he will be told ' from the Tessin '. Now the Tessin is a Swiss valley sloping southwards to the Italian frontier, and though the bees which are found in northern Switzerland are dark, the bees in these southern valleys have the yellow bands of Italian bees. Bees from these Swiss valleys (not from Piedmont or Illyria) were the first to be introduced to other European countries and to the United States. The first introductions were made in two different places almost simultaneously.

A certain Captain Baldenstein, who had served in Italy during the Napoleonic Wars, imported Italian bees and established them at his home in Switzerland in September 1843. His writings attracted the notice of Dzierzon, who received bees from Vienna in 1853 ; the use he made of these bees in establishing his theory of parthenogenesis is well known. Dzierzon's writings inspired Samuel Wagner, the first Editor of the *American Bee Journal*, with the idea of trying these bees in the United States. Wagner and several associates (amongst them Langstroth) attempted to import Italian bees in 1855 and 1858–59, but all the bees died.

However on 18th April 1860 the steamer *Arago* landed in New York with some queens (still alive), which had been sent by a botanist named S. B. Parsons, acting as an agent of the U.S. Government. They had been purchased from H. C. Hermann, who published a book about this race of bees in each of the three Swiss languages : *L'abeille italienne des Alpes* (1860), *Die italienische Alpenbiene* (1859) and *Della coltivazione delle api nella Valtellina* (1860). In 1860 a translation of Hermann's book was published in London under the title *The Italian Alp-bee ; or, The gold mine of husbandry*. There can be little doubt that the bees this man supplied came from the Swiss Alpine valleys.

Meanwhile in England, T. W. Woodbury of Exeter had read the chapter on foreign bees which appeared in Volume VI of the Naturalist's Library, written by the Reverend W. Dunbar, and proceeded in conjunction with Neighbour to import Italian bees ; a few queens reached him in the summer of 1859.

According to Neighbour (1878), the first Carniolan bees were imported into England in 1870 by the Reverend W. C. Cotton ; it seems that Neighbour housed them. Cyprian bees were tried in England after the return from the Middle East of T. B. Blow (founder of the firm of E. H. Taylor, Ltd.) in 1887, but the uncertainty of their temper prevented their gaining popularity.

HIVES AND BEEKEEPING SYSTEMS

The second half of the nineteenth century was marked by a great controversy between the advocates of the old and those of the new systems of beekeeping. There were three protagonists in this controversy, which began in *The Times* and overflowed into other newspapers. The first was Dr. John Cumming, known as The Times Bee Master ; the second was W. B. Tegetmeier, at one time Secretary of the Muswell Hill Beekeepers' Association, and founder of the Library which is now the ' Miller Memorial Library '; the third was T. W. Woodbury, the Devonshire beekeeper who invented the Woodbury movable-comb hive, which in its time was a very good one (see Plate 8, page 77).

The Times Bee Master was a little old-fashioned ; he did not advise the use of the movable frames, which at that time would have been too expensive for the use of the cottagers for whose benefit he was writing. He seems to have been a good beekeeper, for he entirely objected to sulphuring bees, and he was well read in the subject. He strongly believed that his bees knew him. One point in which he was in advance of his time was his advocacy of the Stewarton hive which yielded him large crops of honey at his home in Tunbridge Wells.

Experience shows that acute controversies in beekeeping have arisen at periods when, as in 1864, the methods of working are so to speak in the melting pot; however, acute controversies about things which can only be settled by experience are undesirable, and unrewarding.

Mr. Piers Edgcumbe Martin, Master Mariner, Bee Master, Proprietor and Manager of the Great Hampshire Bee Farm at King's Sombourne, near Stockbridge, Hampshire, was a genius born before his time. In 1878 and 1879 he issued *The bee-keeper's almanac*, which was intended to ensure that those who purchased it became successful beekeepers ; they certainly would have done so if the almanac had continued to forecast the weather as successfully as it did in its first year. In 1878 he issued *The great Hampshire bee farm*, in which he described his patent bar-frame hive, the forerunner of the present standard National hive. This embodied a new and useful idea which was successful in good honey districts. At the proper time nine frames full of comb and brood, together with one empty frame, were added to the brood nest of a hive, and an enormous patent super was placed above. Martin stated that in the height of the season the bees would carry 10 to 12 pounds of honey a day into this hive, which may well have been true ; however the hive was successful only if the conditions were suitable, and foreknowledge of the weather was necessary in order to enable the beemaster to add his supers at the right time.

Samuel Simmins began to write in 1882 when he published his *Facts for bee-keepers, The Simmins method of direct introduction*. This was followed in 1887 by *A modern bee-farm*, of which many editions were sold. The phrase in the title ' £300 per annum from 30 acres ' shows the class of people to which Simmins belonged. His book was severely practical, full of good sense and original ideas ; it was considerably larger than the books by Cowan and Digges, and many beekeepers looked to it as their oracle to which they could always usefully refer. Simmins' hives, however, were not so successful ; they were operated from the back, and the brood boxes and supers were arranged to pull out as from a chest of drawers. This arrangement appealed to beginners, but in practice it was found that the bees propolized the drawers, and this caused trouble.

G. Wells of Aylesford, near Maidstone, was another man in advance of his time. (Such bee men are not always to be commiserated on the failure of their ideas ; this is often due to neglect of sufficient experiment to make their hive or apparatus work satisfactorily before it is put on the market.) Wells hit on the idea of placing two queens in a hive, which is now a common practice. In 1894 he published his *Pamphlet on the two-queen system*. This aroused a great deal of interest and led many people to try his system ; however it did not prove permanently successful. Its importance is that it paved the way for other and more successful two-queen systems.

Reference may be made here to a pamphlet by the Reverend E. Bartrum, Headmaster of Berkhamsted School. It was published in 1881 and entitled *The Stewarton ; the hive of the busy man.* It gives a description of the working of this hive in its latter days, after it had been fitted with frames, and when it was producing the famous honey which carried off so many prizes at the early shows at the Crystal Palace. Plate 7 (page 66) shows one of the plates from the book.

The opportunity may now be taken to give some account of the long history of the Stewarton hive which, as has already been stated, was first produced by Robert Ker in or about 1819. Ker was known as Bee Robin ; he was a good workman, and very fond of bees, and he made many experiments before he put the Stewarton hive on the market. In his old age his sons took him with them to America. The earlier pattern of his hive was fitted with bars across the top of the brood box and of the supers. Other bars, called slides, ran in grooves between these bars, and were removed when it was intended to allow the bees to climb up into the supers. Three generations of the Walker family kept bees in these hives. Robert Walker, the friend of Ker, started to keep bees five years before the death of Robert Burns, and continued for forty-six years after it ; his son continued to use the hives until 1916, and a grandson until 1946. Some of the original supers were in use by the Walker family for 132 years. The sliding bars were replaced by frames shortly before Langstroth invented his movable frames.

It will by now be clear that very many hives of different patterns were on the market during the period between 1850 and 1900 ; the picture in Neighbour's book *The apiary* gives some idea of the variety of patterns offered by that firm alone. The advent of the British Standard Frame in 1882 did much to standardize hives, because those which could not accommodate it gradually disappeared from the market. Finally the hive invented by Mr. W. B. Carr in 1890 (known as the W.B.C. hive) so far replaced all others that its only real rivals were hives closely resembling it but single-walled on two sides with double walls at the front and back. At the present time it is the fashion to decry W.B.C. hives, but when they were first used there was no other hive to equal them, and even after sixty years, the amateur—for whom they were invented—can still find great merits in the W.B.C. hive. Another of W. B. Carr's inventions which is thought little of now, although it represented a real advance when it was first developed, was the ' metal end ' for spacing the combs ; this was invented in 1887, and became the most common method of comb spacing at the end of the century.

Alfred Rusbridge's *Book for bee-keepers* was published in London in 1875, just after the formation of the B.B.K.A. The author's apiary and hive works were at Sidlesham, near Chichester; he made two types of hives, one which contained bar frames, and one which did not. His book began with an account of a visit to the apiary, where the advantages of bee houses were explained. The advice on management which occupied the rest of the book contained nothing very striking, and was in strong contrast to the information to be obtained from another book, *British bee-farming* by J. F. Robinson, published in 1880. Like modern bee farmers, Robinson had no sympathy with the ways of amateurs, and was more practical and ruthless in his attitude to the bees : ' Bees die of starvation after the first of March '. Some of his remarks savour of earlier days. ' Italians swarm more than Blacks '; ' No system which prevents swarming can be successful '; ' Every bee can undertake any work'; ' Foxes eat bees and honey in winter '; ' Mice have never been known to enter a wooden hive ' (this might well be true if the entrances were made differently); ' St. Laurence's day August 10th is the day of Jubilee for the bees, and those who work on that day are called Quakers '. On the whole, professional beekeeping during the closing years of the nineteenth century appears to have been a thriving business, but not yet out of the stage of the ' small man'.

The second half of the century saw the foundation and growth of a number of firms of hive makers. At the Great Exhibitions of 1851 and 1861, Neighbour and Milton — whose firms were founded about 1814 and 1823 respectively—both provided displays which attracted a great deal of attention. Milton's firm soon came to its end, but Neighbour's continued in the front rank until the death of Alfred Neighbour in 1890. During this period some of the chief firms of today were founded — what is now E. H. Taylor Ltd. by T. B. Blow in 1880, Burtt & Son in 1886, and Robert Lee Ltd. in 1862. Keen rivalry resulted from their attempts to produce better hives and accessories.

MINOR BEEKEEPING BOOKS

A number of books about practical beekeeping, though not in the first rank, deserve mention. The most important of these is Cheshire's *Practical bee-keeping*, the first edition of which was published anonymously by the Bazaar and Mart in 1873 (it is not dated, but the British Museum copy bears the stamp 8.De.73). This was Cheshire's first book, and is good, plain and practical. He was up to date in his knowledge, mentioning some contemporary bee books, and concluding with a discussion of Ligurian bees. It is worth studying if only for the light it throws on the development of a great beekeeper.

The Reverend P. V. M. Filleul published *The English bee-keeper* in 1851 under the pseudonym of ' A Country Curate '; this was quite a good book for its time, and went into several editions.

The Reverend J. G. Wood's *Bees, their habits, management and treatment* was published in 1853. The author was famous as a popular lecturer upon scientific subjects, and his book was a well-judged compilation comprising the knowledge and beliefs commonly held at that time.

W. B. Tegetmeier was so long and honourably known as the pigeon expert of *The Field* that it is hard to realize that as long ago as 1860 he was also recognized as an expert beekeeper. During the time when he was engaged in the controversy with the 'Times Bee Master' (p. 85), and when he published his *Bees, hives and honey* (in 1860), he was the Secretary to the Muswell Hill Society of Beekeepers, who were looked upon as the foremost authorities in England at the time. He founded the Library which formed the nucleus of the Miller Memorial Library.

Two other books are K. B. Edwards' *French Bishop's advice to his poor clergy* and Mrs. Helen Glinn's *Bees-wing's advice to bee-keepers*. This is an early example of a bee book written by a lady, and emanated from the quiet country town of Hereford.

Between 1880 and 1890 a large number of small books were written by members of the British Bee-Keepers' Association, for the instruction of their members and also for the benefit of cottagers. These were well written by distinguished beekeepers such as Cowan, Peel, Raynor, Cheshire and Jenyns, but were short tracts rather than serious books and are now mostly forgotten ; they were, however, very useful at the time they were published.

The *Book of bee-keeping* by W. B. Webster, which was published in 1888, may well come at the end of this list of nineteenth-century books. It was not the last published before the century ended, but it was a bright, well written little book with good illustrations, and it was repeatedly republished, living on to be revised and partly rewritten near the middle of the twentieth century.

OTHER BOOKS RELATED TO BEEKEEPING

For many years books on beekeeping had neglected the subject of the production of mead. Several causes combined to produce this situation. The excise authorities did not look upon its manufacture with favour ; cheap wine was readily obtained from France in large quantities ; the standard of beer which was sold on licensed premises had been improved. As a result, mead, which had always been home-produced, was regarded more and more as a member of the class of British wines which were made by cottagers in accordance with rule-of-thumb methods, such as gooseberry or parsnip wine. It was under these conditions that in the 1890s the Reverend G. W. Bancks produced his pamphlets on *Mead and how to make it* and *The production of vinegar from honey*. It speaks well for the traditional reputation of mead that his book reached a third edition in 1898, but there was to be no serious attempt to rehabilitate the mead industry for another fifty years.

Another book which is likely to remain in a class by itself was entitled *On the oxen-born bees of the ancients (Bugonia)* by C. R. Osten-Sacken, which was published at Heidelberg in 1894. The author tries to prove that the ancient belief that bees were produced from the carcasses of dead oxen was due to the fact that large numbers of the fly *Eristalis tenax* are produced when the bodies of oxen are allowed to decay in the open air, and that this fly so resembles bees in appearance that it is easy to mistake a cloud of them for a swarm of bees. The theory is made plausible by the absence of any mention of honey being produced by oxen-born bees, except in the account given by old Mr. Carew of St. Anthony-in-Roseland in Cornwall, which can be found (amongst other places) in Cotton's *My bee book*. But the story, which originated in Egypt, probably owed its long life not to a mistake in the identity of the insects, but to the ignorance of the fact that the large bee in the colony was not a male, but a female which laid eggs and was the mother of the whole community. When this fact became generally known the story of the oxen-born bees died out.

The inevitable reply to Osten-Sacken's book came in the next year (1895), when George B. Buckton published a book on *Eristalis tenax*, in which four pages were devoted to discussing Osten-Sacken's theory.

Mr. T. B. Blow, the energetic founder of the firm of E. H. Taylor Ltd., undertook a journey to the Middle East in order to investigate for himself the qualities of the Cyprian and Palestinian bees about which Frank Benton and D. A. Jones were making glowing reports. His book *A bee-keeper's experience in the East* was published by the B.B.K.A. in 1882 ; another book (actually an enlarged edition of the first), which he himself published from his works at Welwyn in 1887, dealt with the bees of Northern Italy and Carniola. Blow's statement that dark, as well as golden, bees were to be found in Cyprus was strongly challenged recently by a correspondent who keeps bees in the island. The reputation for ferocity which belongs to the Cyprian bees dates from the bees which were brought to England in 1881 or 1882.

A book which may be mentioned here is the third edition of Bevan's *Honey-bee*. This was revised by W. Augustus Munn and published in 1870. Munn and Bevan had been great friends, though there was a great disparity in their ages, and they had agreed that if Munn survived Bevan he should revise the book. Munn brought the book up to date so far as he could but, naturally, much of the old remained; although it is possible to keep a book up to date by frequent revisions, an attempt to modernize a book which has been unchanged for 35 years is not likely to be very successful. So this book is remembered and valued, not so much as the third edition of Bevan's, but because it contains full sketches and particulars of the bar-frame hive which was invented by Munn in 1841, and which was one of the most interesting of the attempts to produce a movable-frame hive before the appearance of Langstroth's.

EPILOGUE

In dealing with the latter half of the nineteenth century an endeavour has been made to show how foundations were then being laid for the improvements which were brought about in the present century ; it may be useful to review them in order to help us to guess what is coming. One feature of the early part of the present century was the rise of professional and side-line beekeeping, which led to a demand for a simplification and a cheapening of the elaborate system then recommended by Cowan and others. For some time this demand was in the ascendant, and the amateurs were also exhorted to use the methods of large-scale beekeepers. It is now being realized that no one system, and no one strain of bees, can be equally successful in all parts of Britain.

The success of artificial insemination of queens makes it possible for the first time to guarantee matings, and this simplifies one of the problems of bee breeding. The increasing cost of hives and equipment may necessitate changes in materials and methods in the future ; considerable changes will become necessary if and when the backward parts of the world adopt the movable-frame hive, because it is the primitive beekeeping in these areas which supplies much of the world's beeswax. Agriculture may well require more honeybees to replace wild bees as pollinators. There are problems of bee diseases still unsolved, and there is now the hazard of poisoning of bees by pest control materials unknown in the last century. All these factors make it seem likely that the present alliance and co-operation between the scientists and the practical beekeepers will be maintained and strengthened as time goes on.

BIBLIOGRAPHY

B indicates that the publication, or another edition of it, is in the Bee Research
Association Library.

CHAPTERS I AND II. BEFORE 1500

B ARMBRUSTER, L. (1926) Der Bienenstand als völkerkundliches Denkmal *Büch. Bienenk.* 8 : 1–147

B —— (1940) Ueber germanische, besonders nordische Imkerei *Büch. Bienenk.* 6 : 1–144

B BERNER, U. (1954) Die alte Bienenzucht Ostdeutschlands und ihrer völker- und stammeskundlichen Grundlagen *Marburg/Lahn : J. G. Herder Institut*

B BONNER, JAMES (1795) A new plan for speedily increasing the number of bee-hives in Scotland . . . *Edinburgh*

BOSWORTH, J. (1858) The history of the Lauderdale Manuscript of King Alfred's Anglo-Saxon version of Orosius *Oxford*

BUTLER, CHARLES (1634) The feminine monarchie *Oxford : W. Turner* 3rd ed.

COX, J. C. (1905) The Royal Forests of England *London : Antiquary's Books*

B DURUZ, R. M. (1953) The honey-pot game *Bee World* 34 : 90–93

B FRASER, H. M. (1942) Early English methods of beekeeping *Bee World* 23 : 34–36, 43–45

B —— (1950) The story of the progress of beekeeping before 1800 *Bee World* 31 : 33–38

B —— (1951) Beekeeping in antiquity *London : University of London Press* 2nd ed.

B —— (1953) Essex bees in the Domesday Book *Yearbook Essex B.K.A.* : 13–15

B GAYRE, G. R. (1948) Wassail ! in mazers of mead *London : Phillimore*

HARROD, H. (1867) Court Rolls of the Manor of Heacham in Norfolk *Archaeologia* 41 : 4

B HERROD-HEMPSALL, W. (1930, 1937) Bee-keeping new and old *London : British Bee Journal*

HESELTINE, G. C. (1930) Selected works of Richard Rolle *London : Longmans, Green & Co.*

IRELAND (1865-1891) [ed. W. N. Harris & others] Ancient Laws and Institutes of Ireland *London : H.M.S.O.*

LAMOND, E. (1890) Walter of Henley's Husbandry *London : Longmans, Green & Co.*

PALLADIUS (1873, 1879; translated 1420) *Early English Text Society : Orig. Ser. No.* 52 & 72

PLOT, R. (1686) The natural history of Staffordshire *Oxford*

B RANSOME, H. (1937) The sacred bee *London : George Allen & Unwin*

ROGERS, J. E. T. (1866) A history of agriculture and prices in England from 1259 to 1793 *Oxford : Clarendon Press*

STRABO (1917, written 7 B.C.) The geography of Strabo (Loeb Classical Library) Vol. II, pp. 261, 263

THORPE, B. [ed.] (1840) Ancient Laws and Institutes of England *London : Record Commission*

Victoria History of the County of Hampshire (1900–1903) Vol. V, p. 455

WALES (1841) [ed. A. Owen] Ancient Laws and Institutes of Wales *London : Record Commission*

WARD, J. (1911) The Roman era in Britain *London : Antiquary's Books*

WATKINS, A. (1920) Early local bee-keeping *Trans. Woolhope Naturalists' Field Club*

WILLIAMS, B. (1850) Account of the officers of a Manor in Oxfordshire *Archaeologia* 33 : 276

CHAPTERS III AND IV. 1500 TO 1700

BEST, HENRY (1641) Rural economy in Yorkshire in 1641, being the farming and account books of H. Best . . . *Durham* 1857 (ed. C. B. Robinson) *Surtees Society* Vol. 33

BLOUNT, SIR THOMAS POPE (1693) Natural history *London : printed for R. Bentley*

BUTLER, CHARLES (1609) The feminine monarchie *Oxford : printed by Joseph Barnes* (2nd ed. 1623; 3rd ed. 1634)

DE RE RUSTICA (1470) ; many editions by various publishers later

ELDINGEN, A. V. (1578) Wahrhaftiger Bericht von Art und Eigenschaften der Immen oder Bienen . . . .

FITZHERBARDE [FITZHERBERT] (1523) The boke of husbandry *London : Richard Pynson*

B FRASER, H. M. (1950) The story of the progress of beekeeping before 1800 *Bee World* 31 : 33–38

GEDDE, JOHN (1675) A new discovery of an excellent method of bee-houses and colonies *London : printed for the author by D. Newman*

GOEDARTIUS [GOEDAERT], J. (1669) Metamorphosis naturalis *Middleburgh*

HARTLIB, SAMUEL (1651) Samuel Hartlib his legacie *London : H. Hills for R. Wodenothe*

—— (1655) The reformed commonwealth of bees . . . *London : printed for Giles Calvert*

HOOKE, ROBERT (1665) Micrographia *London : J. Martin & J. Allestry*

HYLL, THOMAS (1568) The proffitable arte of gardening . . . . *London : imprinted by T. Marshe*

—— (1574) A profitable instruction of the perfite ordering of bees *London : imprinted by Henrie Bynneman*

JACOB, NICKEL (1568) Gründlicher und nützlicher Unterricht von Wartung der Bienen . . . . *Sprottau*

LAWSON, WILLIAM (1618) A new orchard and garden . . . . also [*title page* 1617] The country housewife's garden *London : Bar. Alsop for Roger Jackson*

LEEUWENHOEK, A. VAN (1673) A specimen of some observations made by a microscope contributed by Leeuwenhoek in Holland lately communicated by Dr. Regnerus de Graaf *Phil. Trans.* 8(94) : 6037-6038

—— (1673) The figures of some of Mr. Leeuwenhoek's microscopical observations formerly published, together with their explication *Phil. Trans.* 8(97) : 6116

LEVETT, JOHN (1634) The ordering of bees . . . . *London : printed by Thomas Harper for John Harison*

MAPLET, JOHN (1567) The green forest or naturall history . . . . *London : Denham*

MARKHAM, GERVASE (1614) Cheape and good husbandry . . . . together, with the use, and profit of bees *London : T.S for R. Jackson*

MOUFET, THOMAS (1658) The theater of insects . . . . *published in Topsel* (1658)

PEPYS, SAMUEL (1665) Diary of Samuel Pepys (ed. H. B. Wheatley) *London : Bell* (1903) Vol. 4 p. 408

PLOT, ROBERT (1677) Natural history of Oxfordshire (pages 180–182, 263) *Oxford : printed at the Theater*

—— (1686) Natural history of Staffordshire (pages 385–387) *Oxford : printed at the Theater*

POWER, HENRY (1663) Experimental philosophy, in three books (Vol. II, Observations XI, XVII) *London : Rowcroft, for Martin & Allestry*

PURCHAS, SAMUEL [the elder] (1625) Purchas his pilgrimes *London : W. Stansby for H. Fetherstone*

—— [the younger] (1657) A theatre of politicall flying-insects . . . *London : printed by R.I. for Thomas Parkhurst*

REMNANT, RICHARD (1637) A discourse or historie of bees . . . . *London : printed by Robert Young for Thomas Slater*

B   RUSDEN, MOSES (1679) A further discovery of bees . . . . *London : printed for the author*

SMITH, J. VAN CROWNINSHIELD (1831) An essay on the practicability of cultivating the honey-bee in maritime towns and cities . . . . *Boston : Perkins & Marvin*

B   SOUTHERNE, EDMUND (1593) A treatise concerning the right use and ordering of bees . . . . *London : imprinted by Thomas Orwin for Thomas Woodcocke*

SWAMMERDAM, JAN (1669) Historia insectorum generalis . . . . *Utrecht*

TOPSEL [TOPSELL], EDWARD (1607) The history of four-footed beasts and serpents . . . *London : Jaggard* [2nd ed. (1658) contained Moufet's book]

TUSSER, THOMAS (1573) Fiue hundreth points of good husbandrie *London : for the Assignes of William Seres* [1571 : A hundreth good pointes of husbandrie]

B   WILDMAN, THOMAS (1768) A treatise on the management of bees . . . . *London : printed for the author*

W[ORLIDGE], J. (1669) Systema agriculturae *London : T. Johnson for Samuel Speed*

B   —— (1676) Vinetum Britannicum *London : printed for Thos. Dring*

B   —— (1676) Apiarium, or a discourse on the government and ordering of bees . . . . *London : printed for Thos. Dring*

—— (1677) Systema horticulturae *London : printed for Thos. Dring*

CHAPTER V. 1700 TO 1750

ANONYMOUS (1745) The female monarchy or The natural history of bees. *London : J. Clarke* [pirate edition of Thorley's Melisselogia]

BAILEY, NATHANIEL [ascribed to] (1704) Dictionarium rusticum. *London : printed for James & John Knapton* . . .

BAKER, HENRY (1742) The microscope made easy. *London : printed by R. Dodsley*

BARTON, BENJAMIN SMITH (1793) An enquiry into the question whether the *Apis mellifica* or true honey bee is a native of America. *Trans. Amer. phil. Soc.* 3 : 241–261

BAZIN, G. A. (1744) The natural history of bees. *London : printed for J. & P. Knapton* . . . [English translation of *Histoire naturelle des abeilles*]

BRADLEY, RICHARD (1726) A general treatise of agriculture . . . husbandry and gardening *London : T. Woodward & J. Peele*

COLUMELLA (1745) Of husbandry, in twelve books . . . [English translation] *London : printed for A. Millar*

COOKE, GEORGE [c.1750] The complete English farmer . . . *London*

DERHAM, WILLIAM (1713) Physico-theology . . . *London : Innys*

—— (1724) Observations about wasps and the difference of their sexes. *Phil. Trans.* (382) : 53–

DINSDALE, JOSHUA (1740) The modern art of breeding bees, a Poem *London : printed for Joseph Davidson*

DOBBS, ARTHUR (1750) On bees and their method of gathering wax and honey. *Phil. Trans.* 46 : 536–549

DUBLIN SOCIETY, BY ORDER OF THE (1733) Instructions for managing bees. *Dublin : printed by A. Rhames, Printer to the Dublin Society*

DUDLEY, PAUL (1721) An account of a method lately practised in New England for discovering where bees hive in the woods, in order to get their honey. *Phil. Trans.* 31 : 148–150

JOHN MARTIN (1684) Ein Bienenbüchel . . . *Lauban* [no copy extant; known from Matuschka's reprint of the part on wax]

LAURENCE, JOHN (1726) A new system of agriculture . . . . *London : Woodward*

MARALDI, GIACOMO F. (1712) Observations sur les abeilles. *Mem. Acad. r. Sci.* : 299–335

—— (1742) On bees [*translated and abridged by John Martyn and Ephraim Chambers, Phil. Hist. Mem. R. Acad. Sci.* 4 : 168–177]

MAXWELL, ROBERT (1747) The practical bee-master . . . *Edinburgh : printed for Robert Drummond*

MONTAGUE, PEREGRINE [c.1750] Family pocket book. *London : printed by Henry Coote*

MOORE, SIR JONAS (1703) England's interest, or The Gentleman farmer's friend . . . *London : J. How*

MORTIMER, JOHN (1707) The whole art of husbandry. *London : printed by J. H. for H. Mortlock*

PLUCHE, N. A. DE LA Le spectacle de la nature . . . *Paris*

—— [trans. J. Humphreys] (1733) *London : Davis*

—— [trans. D. Bellamy] (1743) *London*

REID, JOHN (1683) The Scots gard'ner *Edinburgh : printed by David Lindsay and partners*

STELLUTI's edition of Persius (1630) [cont. 'Descrizzione dell'ape'] *Rome*

SWAMMERDAM, JAN (1737/38) Biblia naturae . . . *Leiden* : ed. *Herman Boerhaave*

—— (1758) The book of nature. *London : C. G. Seyffert*

B THORLEY, JOHN (1744) Melisselogia, or The female monarchy *London : printed for the author and sold by N. Thorley*

B WARDER, JOSEPH (1712) The true Amazons . . . *London : John Pemberton*

CHAPTER VI.   1750 TO 1800

B ADAMS, GEORGE (1787) Essays on the microscope . . . *London : published by the author*

ANONYMOUS (no date) The complete English, French and High German vermin killer *printed and sold by the booksellers of London and Westminster*

ANONYMOUS (c.1760) Farmer's wife *London : printed for Alex. Hogg*

ANONYMOUS (1800) A short history of bees . . . *London : printed for E. Newbery* . . .

BONNER, JAMES (1789) The bee-master's companion and assistant *Berwick : J. Taylor*

BROMWICH, BRYAN J'ANSON (1783) The experienced bee-keeper . . . *London : Chas. Dilly*

COOKE, SAMUEL (c.1780) The complete English gardener . . . to which is added The complete bee-master *London : J. Cooke*

DEBRAW, JOHN (1777) Discoveries on the sex of bees . . . *Phil. Trans.* 67 : 15–32

B GÉLIEU, J. DE [trans. C. S. GRAHAM] (1829) The bee preserver . . . *Edinburgh : J. Anderson*

HALE, THOMAS (1756) A compleat body of husbandry *London : printed for T. Osborne and J. Shipton*

HILL, SIR JOHN (1759) The virtues of honey . . . *London*

G

HUNTER, JOHN (1792) Observations on bees *Phil. Trans.* 82 : 128-195
ISAAC, REV. J. (1799) The general apiarian . . . *Exeter*
B KEYS, JOHN (1780) The practical bee-master . . . *London : printed for the author*
B —— (1796) The antient bee-master's farewell . . . *London : G. G. & J. Robinson*
LABAT, JEAN-BAPTISTE (1728) Nouvelle relation de l'Afrique occidentale
LETTSOM, JOHN COAKLEY [2nd ed. 1796] Hints for promoting a Bee Society *London*
MILLS, JOHN (1766) An essay on the management of bees . . . *London : Johnson & Davenport*
MURPHY, ARTHUR (1799) The bees. A poem *London : Rivington*
POLHILL, NATHANIEL (1778) A letter on Mr. Debraw's improvements in the culture of bees *Phil. Trans.* 68 : 107-110
RIEM, JOHANN (1774) Der entlarvte Wildman *Berlin : George Jacob Decker*
RINGSTED, JOSIAH (c.1775) The farmer, comprehending . . . The ordering of bees *London : Dixwell*
B SOODER, M. (1952) Bienen und Bienenhalten in der Schweiz *Basel : G. Krebs*
SWAMMERDAM, JAN (1758) [trans. T. Flloyd] The book of nature or The history of insects *London : C. G. Seyffert*
SYDSERFF, ROBERT (1792) Sydserff's treatise on bees . . . *Salisbury*
B THORLEY, JOHN (1744) Melisselogia . . . *London : sold by N. Thorley*
WELLS, G. (1894) Guide book pamphlet on the two-queen system *Snodland : Gay*
WHITE, STEPHEN (1756) Collateral bee-boxes . . . *London : Davis & Reymers*
WHITE, W[ILLIAM] (1771) A complete guide to the mystery and management of bees *London : printed for the author*
B WILDMAN, DANIEL (1773) A complete guide for the management of bees . . . *London : printed for the author*
B WILDMAN, THOMAS (1768) A treatise on the management of bees . . . *London : printed for the author*

CHAPTER VII. 1800 TO 1850

B BAGSTER, SAMUEL, JR. (1834) The management of bees. With a description of the " ladies' safety hive " *London : Bagster & Pickering*
B BEVAN, EDWARD (1827) The honey-bee . . . *London : Baldwin, Craddock & Joy*
BONNER, JAMES (1789) The bee-master's companion and assistant . . . *Berwick-on-Tweed : J. Taylor*
B —— (1795) A new plan for speedily increasing the number of bee-hives in Scotland . . *Edinburgh : Moir*
BUSCH, WILHELM [1872] Buzz-a-buzz . . . *London & Chester : Griffin & Phillipson* trans. [by W. C. Cotton] of *Schnurrdiburr*
B CHYLINSKI, DOBROGOST (1845) The bee-keeper's manual . . . *London : W. S. Orr*
B [COTTON, WILLIAM CHARLES] [1837] A short and simple letter to cottagers . . . *Oxford : Oxford Apiarian Society*
B COTTON, WILLIAM CHARLES (1842) My bee book *London : Rivington*
—— (1848) A manual for New Zealand beekeepers *Wellington*
DUNBAR, W. (1820) Some observations on the instinct and operations of bees with a description and figure of a glazed bee-hive *Edin. Phil. J.* 3 : 143–148
—— (1821) Observations on bees, made by means of the mirror-hive *Edin. Phil. J.* 4 : 133–138
B [——] (1840) The natural history of bees . . . *Edinburgh : Lizars The Naturalist's Library. Entomology Vol. VI*

B GÉLIEU, JONAS DE (1829) The bee preserver . . . *Edinburgh & London* : *J. Anderson*
       trans. [by Miss C. Stirling Graham]
B GOLDING, ROBERT (1847) The shilling bee book . . . *London* : *Longman, Brown*
   HEWISON, JAMES (1818) An essay on the management of bees *Mem. Caledonian
       Hort. Soc.* 2 : 121–133 [read 13 Dec. 1814]
   HOWATSON, T. M. (1827) The apiarian's manual . . . *Edinburgh* : *Black & Tait*
B HUBER, FRANÇOIS (1806) New observations on the natural history of bees
       Edinburgh : *Anderson* trans. [by Sir J. G. Dalyell]
B —— (1926) New observations upon bees *Hamilton, Ill.* : *American Bee Journal*
       trans. C. P. Dadant
B HUISH, ROBERT (1815) A treatise on the nature, economy and practical management
       of bees . . . *London* : *Baldwin, Craddock & Joy*
   —— [1819] Instructions for using the Huish hive . . . *London* : *Wetton & Jarvis*
B —— [1820] The cottager's manual . . . *London* : *Wetton & Jarvis*
B [JAMES, THOMAS] (1842) Honey-bee and bee books *Quart. Rev.* 71 : 1–54
   JAMESON, ANDREW (1821) A method of constructing bee-hives of wood . . . *Edin.
       Phil. J.* 4 : 109–111
   JOHNSTON, C. W. (1842) The farmer's encyclopaedia . . . *London* : *Longman, Brown*
B [JOHNSTONE, CHRISTIAN ISOBEL] [1829] Scenes of industry . . . *London* : *John Harris*
   JONES, JOHN (1843) The eclectic hive . . . *Hereford* : *Times Office*
   JONES, T. R. (1845) The natural history of animals *London* : *Van Voorst*
B KIRBY, W. (1802) Monographia Apum Angliae . . . *Ipswich & London* : *J. Raw*
B KIRBY, W. & SPENCE, W. (1815–1826) An introduction to entomology . . . *London* :
       Longman
   LAWRENCE, JOHN (1818) A practical treatise . . . on breeding all kinds of domestic
       poultry . . . (4th ed. ' with additions of bees ' . . . *London* : *Sherwood* 1822)
   MACKENZIE, G. S. (1820) Observations respecting the vision of the humble-bee and
       the honey-bee *Edin. Phil. J.* 3 : 67–69
   MILTON, JOHN (1823) The London apiarian guide . . . *London* : *Apiarian Repository*
B —— (1843) The practical bee-keeper . . . *London* : *Parker*
   MOUBRAY, BONINGTON see LAWRENCE JOHN
   MUNN, W. A. (1844) A description of the bar- and frame-hive . . . *London* : *Van
       Voorst*
B NEIGHBOUR, ALFRED (1865) The apiary . . . *London* : *Kent*
B NUTT, THOMAS (1832) Humanity to honey bees . . . *Wisbech* : *Leach*
   PAYNE, J. H. (1832) The cottager's guide . . . *Bury St. Edmunds* : *Suffolk & Norfolk
       Apiarian Society*
B —— (1833) The apiarian's guide . . . *London* : *Simpkin & Marshall* [2nd ed. of above]
B PILE, MATTHEW (1838) The bee cultivator's assistant . . . *Gateshead* : *G. Watson*
   PITT, W. (1796) General view of the agriculture of the County of Stafford *London* :
       G. Nicol
   PLAYFAIR, JAMES Of the care and knowledge of bees . . . *unpublished* 290 pages (date
       unknown)
B RENNIE, JAMES (1830) Insect architecture *London* : *C. Knight* [Vol. I of *The Library
       of entertaining knowledge*]
   RUSSELL, R. (1822) Rara liber *Elgin* : *published by the author*
   SMITH, RICHARD (1839) The cottager's bee-book . . . *Oxford* : *published by the author*
B STRUTHERS, J. (1951) The Stewarton hive *Scot. Beekpr* 27(12) : 239–241 (1951)
   STRUTT, GEORGE (1825) The practical apiarian . . . *Clare, Suffolk* : *Shearcroft*
B TAYLOR, H. (1838) The bee-keeper's manual . . . *London* : *Groombridge*
B TENNENT, J. N. (1951) ' On [*sic*] the care and knowledge of bees ' by James Playfair
       Scot. Beekpr. 27(12) : 236–237
   WHITE, GILBERT (1789) The natural history of Selborne . . . *London* : *B. White*
   WIGHTON, JOHN (1842) The history and management of bees . . . *London* : *Longman*

CHAPTER VIII. 1850 TO 1900

ATTRIDGE, HENRY L. (1890) South African bees and their practical management
     in movable-comb hives *Wynberg* : *Times Office*
AVEBURY, LORD *see* Lubbock, Sir John
B BANCKS, G. W. [1895] Mead and how to make it *Dartford* : *Perry*
B —— (1896) The production of vinegar from honey *Dartford* : *Perry*
BARTRUM, E. (1881) The Stewarton ; the hive of the busy man *London* : *Longman,
     Green & Co.*
BEVAN, EDWARD (rev. W. A. Munn) (1870) The honey-bee, its natural history,
     physiology and management *London* : *J. van Voorst*
BLOW, T. B. (1882) A bee-keeper's experience in the East *London* : *read to the
     B.B.K.A. April 12th*
—— (1887) A bee-keeper's experience in the East. Among the queen-raisers in the
     North of Italy and Carniola *Welwyn, Herts.* : *T. B. Blow*
BUCKTON, GEORGE B. (1895) The natural history of *Eristalis tenax* of the drone fly
     London : *Macmillan*
B [CHESHIRE, F. R.] [1873] Practical bee-keeping *London* : *Bazaar & Mart*
B —— [1886] Bees and bee-keeping ; scientific and practical   Vol. I—Scientific
     London : *L. Upcott Gill*
B —— (1888) Bees and bee-keeping ; scientific & practical Vol. II—Practical *London* :
     L. Upcott Gill
—— & CHEYNE, W. WATSON (1885) The pathogenic history under cultivation of a
     new bacillus (*B. alvei*) *J.R. micr. Soc.* 5 : 581–601
COTTON, W. C. (1848) Manual for New Zealand beekeepers *Wellington*
B COWAN, T. W. [1881] The British bee-keeper's guide book *London* : *Houlston &
     Sons*
B —— [1890] The honey bee : its natural history, anatomy, and physiology *London* :
     Houlston & Sons
DOUGLAS, JOHN C. (1883) A collection of papers on bee-keeping in India *Calcutta* :
     Government of India
—— (1884) A hand-book of bee-keeping for India *Calcutta*
—— (1886) The hive-bees indigenous to India and the introduction of the Italian
     bee *J. Asiat. Soc. Beng.* No. 3(2) : 83–96
DZIERZON, JOHANN (1848) Theorie und Praxis des neuen Bienenfreundes . . . pub-
     lished by the author
B —— (1882) Rational bee-keeping *London* : *Houlston & Sons* (trans. H. Dieck & S.
     Stutterd, ed. C. N. Abbott)
B EDWARDS, K. B. (1878) French bishop's advice to his poor clergy *Burbage* :
     Hinckley
B [FILLEUL, P. V. M.] (1851) The English bee-keeper *London* : *F. & J. Rivington*
GILLIES, J. M. (1895) Stepping-stones to bee-keeping *Dublin* : *M. H. Gill & Son*
GLINN, HELEN (1876) Bees-wing's advice to bee-keepers *Hereford* : *Hereford Times*
HERMANN, H. C. (1859) Die italienische Alpenbiene *Chur* : *Leonhard Hitz*
—— (1860) L'abeille italienne des Alpes *Chur* : *Senti & Hummel*
—— (1860) Della coltivazione delle api nella Valtellina *Milan* : *Vallerdi*
—— (1860) The Italian Alp-bee ; or, The gold mine of husbandry *London* : *Neighbour*
B HOPKINS, ISAAC (1881) The illustrated New Zealand bee manual *Thames Goldfield* :
     Advertiser Office

—— (1886) The illustrated Australasian bee manual . . . *Auckland : Gordon & Gotch* [?]

JONES, H. P. & MICHAEL, D. (1888) Y gwenynydd *Bala*

B LANGSTROTH, L. L. (1853) The hive and the honey-bee *Northampton, Mass. : Hopkins, Bridgman & Co.*

LOWE, JOHN (1867) Observations on Dzierzon's theory of reproduction in the honey-bee *Trans. Ent. Soc. Ser.3 5 : 547–560*

B LUBBOCK, SIR JOHN (1882) Ants, bees and wasps *London : Kegan Paul, Treuch & Co.*

—— (1888) On the senses, instincts and intelligence of animals with special reference to insects *London : Kegan Paul, Trench & Co.*

MACKENZIE, JOHN (1860) The management of bees *Edinburgh & London : Blackwood*

MARTIN, PIERS EDGCUMBE (1878, 1879) The bee-keeper's almanac . . . *London : Simpkin, Marshall & Winchester : Tanner & Sons*

—— (1878) The great Hampshire bee farm *London : Simpkin Marshall & Winchester : Tanner & Sons*

B NEIGHBOUR, A. (1878) The apiary ; or bees, bee-hives, and bee-culture (3rd ed. p. 45) *London : Kent & Co.*

OSTEN-SACKEN, C. R. (1894) On the oxen-born bees of the ancients (Bugonia) and their relation to *Eristalis tenax*, a two-winged insect *Heidelberg : J. Hoerning*

PAGDEN, J. W. [1868] £70 a year ; how I make it by my bees and how a cottager or other may soon do the same [?] *Alfriston, Sussex : published by the author*

B PELLETT, F. C. (1938) History of American beekeeping *Ames, Iowa : Collegiate Press*

PRATT, Mrs. J. B. (1853) The bee and bee-keeper's friend *Aberdeen : L. & J. Smith*

B ROBINSON, J. F. (1880) British bee-farming : its profit and pleasures *London : Chapman & Hall*

ROMANES, GEORGES J. (1882) Animal intelligence *London : Kegan Paul, Trench & Co.*

B ROOT, A. I. (1877) The ABC of bee culture . . . *Medina, Ohio : A. I. Root*

RUSBRIDGE, ALFRED (1875) A book for bee-keepers, showing . . . net profit 100 to 300 per cent annually on capital invested, in keeping bees *London : E. W. Allen*

B —— (1883) Bee-keeping plain and practical and how to make it pay *London : E. W. Allen*

B SAMUELSON, JAMES & HICKS, J. BRAXTON (1860) The honey-bee, its natural history, habits, anatomy and microscopical beauties *London : J. van Voorst*

B SHUCKARD, W. E. (1866) British bees *London : Lovell Reeve*

B SIEBOLD, C. T. E. VON (1857) On a true parthenogenesis in moths and bees *London : J. van Voorst* (trans. W. S. Dallas)

B SIMMINS, SAMUEL [1882] Facts for bee-keepers. The Simmins method of direct introduction . . . *London : published by the author*

B —— (1887) A modern bee-farm and its economic management *London : Pettitt*

[TEGETMEIER, W. B.] [1860] Bees, hives and honey *London : W. Allan & Co.* [?]

B WEBSTER, W. B. [1888] Book of bee-keeping *London : L. Upcott Gill* (7th ed. [1938])

WELLS, G. (1894) Guide book pamphlet on the two-queen system *Snodland : Gay*

B WOOD, J. G. (1853) Bees, their habits, management and treatment *London : Routledge*

INDEX

Figures in bold type refer to an illustration opposite the page ; figures in italics refer to the bibliography.

Entries are included for names of authors, but not for titles of books except those whose authors are unknown. Places in England are indexed under their counties, and those in Ireland, Scotland, Wales, and countries overseas, are indexed under country.

Lightning Source UK Ltd.
Milton Keynes UK
UKOW02f1836180614

233682UK00001B/14/P